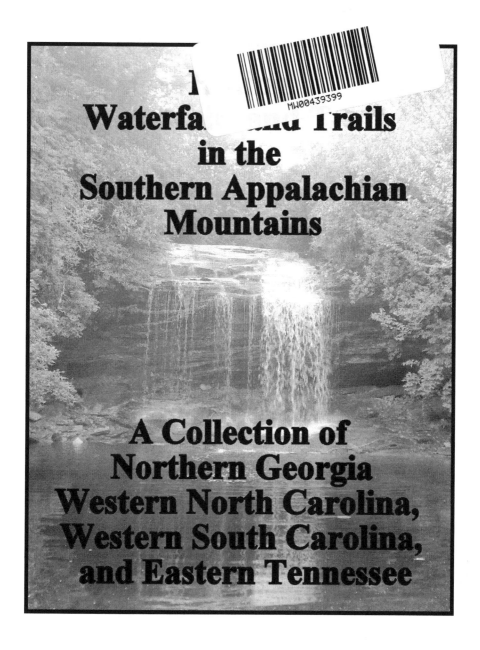

Waterfalls and Trails
in the
Southern Appalachian Mountains

A Collection of
Northern Georgia
Western North Carolina,
Western South Carolina,
and Eastern Tennessee

Jack M. Ellison

KINDLE/KDP/AMAZON
INDEPENDENT PUBLISHING

ISBN 9781731291882

Edited by Edna Ellison, PhD.

www.ednaellison.net

Page Editor Vickie H. Holt

Dedication

I want to dedicate this book to our Lord and Savior, Jesus Christ, without whom we would not be able to enjoy these great trails. "For God so loved the world that He gave his one and only Son, that whoever believes in Him shall not perish but have eternal life" (John 3:16 NIV).

Table of Contents
Georgia

41   North Carolina

7

101   South Carolina

125   Tennessee

137   About the Author

GEORGIA

Hiking Trails in
Northern Georgia

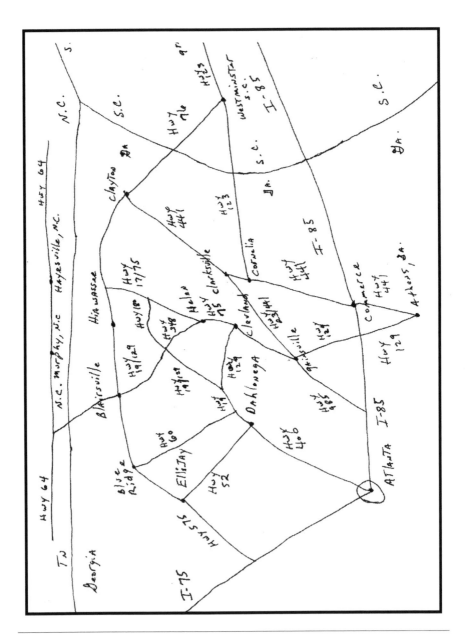

BLAIRSVILLE:
BRASSTOWN BALD, GA

Length of Trail: .5 miles one way
Type of Trail: Out and Back
Condition of Trail: Excellent. Paved
Difficulty of Trail: Moderate
Approx Hiking Time: 1 hr
Directions to Trailhead: From Blairsville, Georgia, take US 19 &
129 south for 8 miles. Turn left (east) onto Georgia hwy 180. Go 9
miles to Georgia Spur 180 and turn left (north). Go 3 miles to the
Brasstown Bald parking lot.
Trail Description: From the Gift Shop take the summit Trail, a steep
half mile to the observation deck and museum.

DESOTO FALLS, GA

Length of Trail: 1.1 miles one way
Type of Trail: Out and Back to both falls. T shaped
Condition of Trail: Good
Difficulty of Trail: Easy to Moderate
Approx Hiking Time 1.5 to 2 hrs.
Directions to Trailhead: From the intersection of hwy 19/129 in
Turner's Corner, GA, take hwy 19 north for approx 4 miles to
Desoto Recreation Area on the left. There is a small parking fee.
Trail Description: From the parking area walk through the camping
/picnic area to the bridge over Frogtown Creek. After crossing the
bridge, take a left to the Lower Falls at .3 mile. Backtrack to the
footbridge and continue straight ahead another .8 mile to the new
Upper Falls. [The new Upper Falls used to be the Middle Falls
before the old Upper Falls were closed, due to safety reasons.] After
viewing the falls, return to the Trailhead, giving you a total of 2.2
miles roundtrip.

HELTON CREEK FALLS, GA

Length of Trail: .2 mile one way
Type of Trail: Out and Back
Condition of Trail: Good
Difficulty of Trail: Easy
Approx Hiking Time: 30 minutes
Directions to Trailhead: From Blairsville, GA head south on US hwy
19/129 for 11 Miles to Helton Creek Rd (FS 118), on the left just
past the entrance to Vogel State Park. Take Helton Creek Rd for 2.2
miles to the parking area on your right.
Trail Description: From the parking area, take the Helton Creek Falls
trail .1 mile to a side trail that leads to the lower falls. After viewing,
return to the main trail and continue to the base of the upper falls and
observation area at .2 mile. Return the way you came.

SEA CREEK FALLS

Sea Creek Falls: Suches, GA
Length of Trail: .2 mile one way
Type of Trail: Out and Back
Condition of Trail: Good
Difficulty of Trail: Easy
Approx Hiking Time: less than 30 minutes
Direction to the Trailhead: From the intersection of GA hwy 60/180 in Suches, GA, drive north on hwy 60 for 10.8 miles to the sign for Cooper Creek Scenic Area. Do not turn on the first Cooper Creek Rd. Turn right on to FS4 and go approx 3 miles to FS 264 just before the Sea Creek ford. Take a left on FS 264 and go .3 mile to the trailhead for Sea Creek Falls.
Trail Description: From the parking area, follow the trail upstream along the creek .2 mile to reach the falls. Return the way you came.

BLUE RIDGE:
BENTON MACKAYE TRAIL (SECTION 2)
HWY 60 TO SUSPENSION BRIDGE

Length of Trail: 3.5 miles one way
Type of Trail: Out and Back
Condition of Trail: Good
Difficulty of Trail: Moderate
Approx Hiking Time: 4-5 hrs
Directions to Trailhead: From Morganton, GA travel south on GA hwy 60 approx 12 miles to where the Benton MacKaye Trail crosses the road. Parking is on the left.
Trail Description: Walk across the road onto the BMT. Trail gradually ascends Tooni Mountain. Crosses old roadbed at 3.3 miles. That leads to the right. Reach Suspension Bridge at approx 3.5 miles. Return the way you came.

BENTON MACKAYE TRAIL (BMT) SECTION 9

Length of Trail: 7.8 miles, including a 3.3 mile walk on FS64 to close the loop.
Type of Trail: Loop
Condition of Trail: Good
Difficulty of Trail: Moderate to Strenuous due to length.
Approx Hiking Time 4-5 hrs
Directions to Trailhead: From the intersection of US76/GA5/GA2 in Blue Ridge, GA at McDonalds take GA5 north approx 3.7 miles to Old GA hwy 2. Follow Old State Rte 2, 10.3 miles to Watson Gap. Pavement ends at approx 9 miles. Park at Watson Gap.
Trail Description: From Watson Gap walk south on FS64 toward Dyer Gap for a little less than a hundred yards. Trail will go off in the woods to the right. At 2.3 miles it intersects the south fork trail. The 2 trails share the next 1.6 miles to mile 3.9 where the 2 trails split. Take the BMT left and follow a small branch upstream. At mile 4.4 turn left onto FS64. Head North on FS64 to mile 4.5 at Dyer Gap at the 3-way intersection of FS64 and FS64A. Continue North on FS64 for 3.3 miles, passing Dyer Mountain Cemetery, continuing back to Watson Gap to close the loop, and completing the 7.8 mile loop.

FLATCREEK LOOP

Length of Trail: 5.8 miles including connector trail.
Type of trail: Loop
Condition of Trail: Good
Difficulty of Trail: Moderate
Approx Hiking Time: 3-3.5 hrs
Directions to Trailhead: From McDonald's restaurant at intersection of GA hwy 515 and GA hwy 5 in Blue Ridge, proceed east on GA hwy 515 (toward Blairsville), approx. 0.8 miles to Windy Ridge Rd. At Windy Ridge Rd, turn right, go 0.2 miles to dead end at Old U.S. 76. Turn left, go 0.2 miles to Aska Rd on right. Turn right, go south 4.4 miles to Deep Gap parking area below gap and on right side of road.
Trail Description: From the Deep Gap parking area, head up the Flatcreek Trail approx .5 mile, to the loop part of the trail. Go either direction and it will bring you back to this point, after walking the loop. Very pleasant, beautiful woods, and a creek. Good fall or winter hike.

GREEN MOUNTAIN TRAIL
DEEP GAP BLUE RIDGE, GA.

Length of Trail: 3.3 miles one way
Type of Trail: Out and Back
Condition of Trail: Good
Difficulty of Trail: Moderate
Approx Hiking Time: 3.5-4.5 hrs
Directions to Trailhead: From McDonald's restaurant at intersection of GA hwy 515 and hwy 5 in Blue Ridge, proceed east on GA hwy 515 (toward Blairsville) approx. 0.8 mile to Windy Ridge Rd. At Windy Ridge Rd turn right, go 0.2 mile to dead end with Old US 76. Turn left, go 0.2 mile to Aska Road on right. Turn right, go south 4.4 miles to Deep Gap parking area below the gap on right side of road.
Trail Description: Take the trail directly across the street from the Deep Gap parking area. Walk .8 mile to the old intersection of the lower and the upper Green Mt. Trails. The trail to the left has been decommissioned. Continue straight or to the right, to mile 1.3 at a signed junction with the .5 mile connector trail to Long Branch Loop. Continue to the left here to stay on the Green Mt. Trail. The trail starts losing elevation heading toward the lake, ties into an old roadbed at 2.3 miles and starts following the shoreline of the lake at 2.6 to 3.3 miles. Return the way you came.

CLAYTON:

BECKY BRANCH FALLS
via Bartram Trail at Warwoman Dell

Length of Trail: .2 miles one way
Type of Trail: Out and Back
Approx Hiking Time: 15-20 minutes   Condition of Trail: Good
Difficulty of Trail: Easy to Moderate. Due to steepness of the trail up
to Becky Branch Falls.
Directions to the Trailhead: Warwoman Dell is located on
Warwoman Rd, 2.8 miles east of where that road intersects US hwy
441 in downtown Clayton, GA. After taking a right into Warwoman
Dell, follow the road all the way to the end to the parking/picnic
area. To access the Trailhead, walk back down the road you came in
on and take a left on The Bartram Trail, near an information kiosk
describing the old Fish Hatchery.
Trail Description: From the Trailhead, hike north on the Bartram
Trail. At .1 mile, reach Warwoman Rd. Cross the road but be careful
and look both ways before crossing; it can be busy. Ascend uphill
at .2 miles to the observation area on the footbridge at the base of
Becky Branch Falls. Return the way you came.

BECKY BRANCH FALLS
via Bartram Trail at Warwoman Dell
Continued

Becky Branch Falls via Bartram Trail

DICK'S CREEK FALLS AND LEDGE ON THE CHATTOOGA RIVER

Length of Trail:
1.7 miles
Type of Trail: Loop
Condition of Trail: Good
Difficulty of Trail: Easy to
Moderate
Hiking Time: 1-2 hrs
Directions to Trailhead: From
the intersection of hwy 441
and Warwoman Rd in Clayton, GA, take Warwoman Rd 5.9 miles to
Sandy Ford Rd on the right. Take Sandy Ford Rd .6 miles, staying
left at the intersection with John Houck Rd, where the road turns to

gravel and crosses
Warwoman Creek.
Continue on Sandy
Ford Rd another 3.4
miles, totaling 4 mi.
from Warwoman Rd,
and park just before the
road fords Dick's Creek.
Trail Description: Take
the trail that runs along
the left side of Dick's
Creek. At .5 mile, cross

the Bartram and Chattooga River Trails, and continue over a
footbridge to Dick's Creek Falls at .6 miles. Continue on Dick's
Creek Trail to .7 mile, reaching the Chattooga River and Dick's
Creek Ledge. After viewing the falls and the river, backtrack .2 mile
at .9 mile to the Bartram Trail. Take a left, heading back toward
Sandy Ford Rd and Bartram Trail intersection. At 1.3 miles, the
Bartram Trail and Chattooga River Trails split. The Chattooga River
Trail goes left. Stay right on the Bartram Trail all the way back to
Sandy Ford Rd at 1.4 miles. Take a right on Sandy Ford Rd and walk
back to your car at 1.7 miles.

HOLCOMB CREEK AND
AMMONS CREEK FALLS, GA

Length of Trail: 2 miles
Type of Trail: Loop
Condition of Trail: Good. Rough in some spots.
Difficulty of Trail: Moderate
Approx Hiking Time: 2-2.5 hrs
Directions to the Trailhead: From the intersection of hwy 441 and
Warwoman Rd in Clayton, GA take Warwoman Rd approx.10 miles
to Hale Ridge Rd (FS7) on the left. Take Hale Ridge Rd 7 miles to
its intersection with Overflow Rd (FS 86). There is parking on the
right just before this intersection. Across from the intersection is the
trailhead, marked with a blue band around a tree and a large boulder
engraved with "Holcomb Creek Trail." An alternate trailhead can be
found by taking a left at this intersection on Hale Ridge Rd and
continuing another .6 mile to the trailhead on the right, past the
bridge.
Trail Description: From the boulder marking the trailhead, walk
down the trail, arriving at Holcomb Creek Falls and an observation
deck at .3 mile. Continue on the trail, bypass your return route on the
left before reaching Ammons Creek Falls and observation deck at .5
mile. After viewing the falls, backtrack a short distance to Holcomb
Creek Trail on the right. Take this trail, making this a loop. To view
a water slide on Holcomb Creek trail at approx 1 mile, continue on
to the alternate trailhead and Hale Ridge Rd (FS7) at 1.4 miles. Take
a left on Hale Ridge Rd and return to your car at 2 miles.

MINNEHAHA FALLS TRAIL

Length of Trail: .3 mile one way
Type of Trail: Out and Back
Condition of Trail: Good
Difficulty of Trail: Easy
Approx Hiking Time: 30-45 minutes
Directions to Trailhead: From Tallulah Falls, GA, take hwy 441
North toward Clayton. After crossing the Tallulah Falls Bridge, go
1.7 miles and turn Left onto Old hwy 441. Proceed 2.5 miles and
turn left onto Lake Rabun Rd. Travel 5 miles to Rabun Beach
Campground.
From the Rabun Beach Campground # 2 entrance, continue west on
Lake Rabun Road for 1.6 miles. Turn left and cross the bridge on
Low Gap Rd and go .2 mile. Make another left onto Bear Gap Road
and proceed 1.6 miles to the Minnehaha Trail on the right. Parking is
on the left, near the trailhead, and is very limited, to 3-4 vehicles.
Trail Description: Follow the trail .3 mile to the falls. This is a very
pleasant walk, slightly uphill, but not difficult.

RABUN BALD, GA

Length of Trail 1.7 miles one way
Type of Trail: Out and Back
Condition of Trail: Good
Difficulty of Trail: Moderate
Approx Hiking Time: 3-3.5 hrs
Directions to Trailhead: Take US 441 north from Dillard, GA, for 1 mile. Turn right onto GA 246 toward Highlands, NC; continue on GA 246, which turns into NC 106, for 7 miles; turn right onto Hale Ridge Road (FS 7), which is beside the Scaly Post Office. Go 2.1 miles and take the right fork on Bald Mountain Rd (FS 7 goes left); and go 1.2 miles and take a left on Kelsey Mountain. Rd and go .3 mile to Bee Gum Gap. Be sure not to block any driveways or gated roads. There is limited parking here. Park beside the road.
Trail Description: From the parking area beside the road at Bee Gum Gap, walk up the old 4-wheel-drive road for approx 1 mile to the end of the road and the intersection of the Bartram Trail. Take the Bartram Trail to the right (north) another .7 mile to the observation deck on Rabun Bald with 360-degree views.

DAHLONEGA:
AMICALOLA FALLS LOOP

Length of Trail: Approx 2 miles
Type of Trail: Loop
Condition of Trail: Good
Approx Hiking Time: 2 to 2.5 hrs, depending on how much time you spend at the falls.
Directions to the Trailhead: From Dahlonega, GA, take hwy 52 west /GA 9 south for approx 4 miles to hwy 52 west. Take a right and follow for approx 14 miles to Amicalola Falls State Park. From the entrance, go past the ranger's residence and park in the Appalacian Trail (AT) parking lot across from the Visitor Center.
Trail description: From the parking area, follow the creek trail (parallel to the road) to join the AT Approach Trail, or follow the AT Approach Trail behind the visitor center (that runs parallel to the road), upward to the lower observation deck. Take West Ridge Staircase, approx 800 steps to the Falls Overlook at approx 1 mile. From the Falls Overlook take the East Ridge Trail back to the Visitor Center and parking area to complete the loop at approx 2 miles.

Hike Inn /Approach Trail Loop,
Amicalola Falls State Park, GA

Length of Trail: 10 miles
Type of Trail: Loop
Condition of Trail: Good
Difficulty of Trail: Strenuous
Approx Hiking Time: 6.5 hrs
Directions to the Trailhead: From Dahlonega, GA, take hwy 52 west /GA 9 south for approx 4 miles to hwy 52 west. Turn right, drive approx 14 miles to Amicalola Falls State Park. From entrance, go past ranger's residence, and right before the Visitor Center, take a left on paved road that leads up to the parking area, with an overlook at the top of Amicalola Falls. Park here. If you have time, it is a good idea to go into the Visitor Center and get a map of the park.
Trail Description: From the parking area at the top of the falls, take the Appalachian Approach Trail/Hike Inn Trail; they share the same path for approx   .3 miles before the Hike Inn Trail splits off to the right. Take the Hike Inn Trail another 4.5 miles to reach the Hike Inn. After checking out the Hike Inn, continue approx. another mile reaching the AT Approach Trail at Mile 5.8 between Frosty Mountain and Nimblewill Gap. Take a left on the Approach Trail (south) and continue another 4.25 miles back to the Trailhead, giving you a total of about a 10-mile loop.

AT (APPALACHIAN TRAIL)
BMT (BENTON MACKAYE TRAIL, Section 1)
Double Loop, the closest 2 loops to Springer Mountain

Length of trail: 6.2 miles
Type of Trail: Loop
Condition of Trail: Good
Difficulty of Trail: Moderate
Approx Hiking Time: 3-4 hrs
Directions to Trailhead: From Blue Ridge, GA, go south on Aska
Road to its end (13.5 miles). Turn right on Newport Road, and go
4.5 miles. Turn right onto Doublehead Gap Road; go 2.0 miles to
(unmarked) USFS Road 42 on left (Mt. Pleasant Church on right).
Turn onto USFS 42, drive 6.5 miles to the AT crossing of Forest
Road 42 and parking lot on left.

AT / BENTON MACKAYE TRAIL
Continued

Trail Description: From the AT on FS42 near Springer Mt., hike the AT south .9 mile to the top of Springer Mt. After enjoying the view, backtrack north on the AT for .2 mile to the BMT. Head east (north) on the BMT, reaching Owen's Overlook on a side path at 1.4 miles from the start of the BMT. Continue to Big Stamp Gap, crossing FS42 at 1.8 miles on the BMT or 2.9 miles total. Continue west (north) on the BMT to a junction with the AT, at 3.2 miles on the BMT or 4.3 miles total. Continue heading north on the BMT to another junction of the AT, at 3.9 miles on the BMT or 5 miles total. From this intersection, head south on the AT to reach a previous intersection with the BMT and close the top (smaller) loop at 5.6 miles total. Continue south on the AT another .6 miles to the FS42 parking lot to complete the bottom 2 loops on the AT/BMT at 6.2 miles.

ELLIJAY:
PANTHER CREEK FALLS, Cohutta Wilderness, GA

Length of Trail: 4.3 miles one way. 8.6 miles roundtrip
Type of Trail: Out and Back
Condition of Trail: Good. Rough in some spots.
Difficulty of Trail: Strenuous / Approx Hiking Time: 5-6 hrs
Directions to Trailhead: From Ellijay, GA, take hwy 52 West
towards Chatsworth, GA, for a little over 5 miles to Gates Chapel Rd
on the right. Take Gates Chapel Rd for Approx 7 miles to the
intersection of FS90/FS68. After about 5.5 miles, Gates Chapel Rd
becomes gravel and turns into FS 90. At the intersection FS90/FS68,
turn to the right and uphill on FS 68 headed toward Lake Conasauga
and the wilderness area. Stay on FS 68 for approx 3.5 miles to the 3-
way FS68/FS64 intersection at Potatopatch Mountain. Take a right
on FS 64 and travel approx 4.3 miles to the Three Forks Trailhead.
Trail Description: From the Three Forks Trailhead, head north on the
East Cowpen Trail for 2.4 miles to the intersection of the Panther
Creek Trail on the left. Take the Panther Creek Trail west for approx
1.9 miles to Panther Creek Falls and Bluff, with an open view of the
wilderness. Return the way you came.

HELEN:

ANNA RUBY FALLS, GA

Length of Trail: .4 mile one way
Type of Trail: Out and Back
Condition of Trail: Excellent: Paved
Difficulty of Trail: Easy, Moderate near the end
Directions to Trailhead: From Helen, GA, head north on GA hwy 75
for approx 1 mile and turn right onto GA 356 East. Drive 1.3 miles
and take a slight left onto Anna Ruby Falls Rd and go 3.5 miles.
Turn left to stay on Anna Ruby Falls Rd to the end of the road and
parking lot to the Anna Ruby Falls Visitor Center and Gift Shop.
Trail Description: Take the paved trail .4 mile to the falls. Easy
walk in the beginning. Gets steeper near the end. Has several
observation decks.

DUKE'S CREEK FALLS, GA

Length of Trail: 1.1 mile one way
Type of Trail: Out and Back
Condition of Trail: Good
Approx Hiking Time: 1-2 hrs
Difficulty of Trail: Easy to Moderate

Directions to Trailhead: Take GA 75 north from Helen for 1.5 miles. Turn left on GA 75 Alternate for 2.3 miles to the Richard Russell Scenic Highway 348. Turn right, go 2 miles to Duke's Creek Falls Recreation Area on the left. There is a small parking fee.
Trail Description: Follow the paved and popular trail .1 mile, to a viewing deck with a long-range view of Duke's Creek Falls. It's another mile to the base of the falls and viewing decks at 1.1 miles. After viewing the falls, return for a round trip of 2.2 miles.

HIGH SHOALS AND BLUE HOLE FALLS, GA

Length of Trail: 1.2 miles one way
Type of Trail: Out and Back
Condition of Trail: Good
Difficulty of Trail: Moderate
Approx Hiking Time: 2 hrs

Directions to Trailhead: From Unicoi Gap on hwy 17/75 north of Helen, GA travel 2 miles north on hwy 17/75 to FS 283 on the right. Take FS 283, Indian Grave Gap Rd, and in a few hundred yards, ford a small stream. Normally this is an easy ford in most vehicles unless the water level is very high. Continue on FS 283 to mile 1.4 and the

High Shoals Scenic Area Trailhead on the left. Park here.
Trail Description: The trail heads north and starts descending downhill into a cove. At .5 mile, reach High Shoals Creek, crossing several bridges and walking the forest floor. At approx 1 mile, reach

a side trail on the left to an observation deck that leads to the base of Blue Hole Falls. After viewing the falls, backtrack to the main trail and continue heading north to mile 1.2 and a side trail to the left that leads to an observation deck at the base of High Shoals Falls. After viewing the falls, return the way you came for a round trip of 2.4 miles.

HORSE TROUGH FALLS IN HELEN, GA

Length of Trail: .15 mile one way
Condition of Trail: Good
Difficulty of Trail: Easy
Approx Hiking Time: 10-15 minutes
Directions to Trailhead: Take GA 75/17 north from Helen for approx 9 miles. Approx 2.5 miles past Andrews Cove campground (after mile marker 15 but before Unicoi Gap) turn left onto Forest Service Road 44 (Wilkes Creek Road). The road is gravel with pull-outs. After approx 4.5 miles into the drive, the Upper Chattahoochee campground is on the right. Turn in and wind your way to the far end of the campground to the day use parking area. A brown sign marks the start of the trail.
Trail Description: From the parking area soon take the trail over a wooden bridge over the Chattahoochee River, only a few feet wide at this point, and continue to follow Horse Trough Creek .15 mile to the falls.

RAVEN CLIFF FALLS, GA

Raven Cliff Falls, GA
Length of Trail: 2.5 miles one way
Type of Trail: Out and Back
Condition of Trail: Good. Can be a little rough as the cove narrows
near Raven Cliff Falls
Difficulty of Trail: Moderate
Approx Hiking Time: 4-5 hrs
Directions to Trailhead: From Helen, take GA 75 north for 1.5 miles.
Turn left on GA 75 Alternate for 2.3 miles to the Richard Russell
Scenic Highway 348. Turn right, go 2.8 miles to Raven Cliff Falls
Recreation Area on the left.
Trail Description: From the large parking area, follow the trail
upstream along Dodd Creek with several nice waterfalls and slides at
.4 mile to 1 mile on the left. Continue upstream to one of the most
impressive falls on Dodd Creek at 1.5 miles. Continue on the trail as
the cove narrows into a ravine, reaching Raven Cliff Falls at approx
2.5 miles. After viewing the falls, return the way you came to
complete a roundtrip of 5 miles.

TRAY MOUNTAIN SUMMIT

Length of Trail: Approx .8 miles one way
Type of Trail: Out and Back
Condition of Trail: Good
Difficulty of Trail: Moderate
Approx Hiking Time: 2-2.5 hrs, depending on how long you
enjoy the views.
Directions to Trailhead: From Helen GA, take GA 75 north for 11
miles, 2 miles north of Unicoi Gap, to FS 283 on the right. Take FS
283 4 miles, past Indian Grave Gap and the AT, and take a left on FS
79 and go 2 miles to the junction of FS 698 and the AT at Tray Gap.
Trail Description: From Tray Gap, head north on the AT .8 mile
uphill to the Tray Mountain Summit for great views.

HIAWASSEE:
DICK'S CREEK GAP

Dick's Creek Gap on AT to view on Powell Mountain
Length of Trail: 2.6 miles one way
Type of Trail: Out and Back
Condition of Trail: Good
Difficulty of Trail: Moderate to Strenuous

Dick's Creek Gap on AT to view on Powell Mountain, Continued

Approx Hiking Time: 3-3.5 hrs, depending on how long you enjoy the view.
Directions to Trailhead: From intersection of GA 17/75 AND hwy 76 Near Hiawassee, GA. Take hwy 76 East approx 7.5 miles to Dick's Creek Gap and the AT parking lot on the left.
Trail Description: From the AT parking lot cross hwy 76 and head south on the AT. At mile 1.2, reach Moreland Gap. Continue uphill, climbing to the top of Powell Mountain at 2.2 miles. At 2.4 miles cross McClure Gap, and at 2.6 miles on the Ridgecrest, a Blue Blazed trail goes east to a campsite and a great view of Lake Burton.

NORTH CAROLINA

Hiking Trails in
Western North Carolina

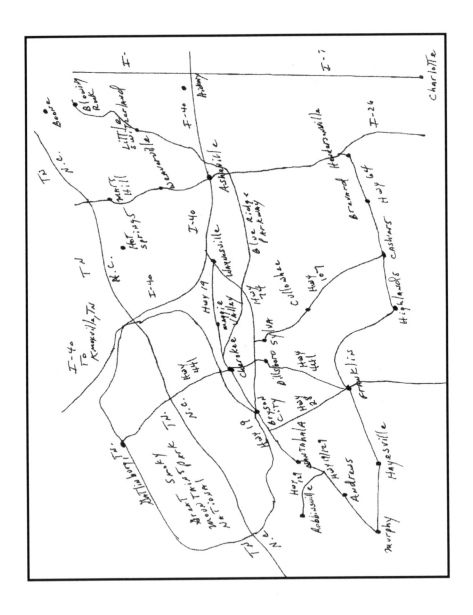

ASHEVILLE:
MOUNT MITCHELL SUMMIT TRAIL

Length of Trail: .25 mile one way
Type of Trail: Out and Back
Condition of Trail: Excellent. Paved
Difficulty of Trail: Easy
Approx Hiking Time: 10-15 minutes
Directions to Trailhead: From the Blue Ridge Parkway milepost
355.3, take NC hwy 128 all the way to the end to the Summit
parking area and Visitor Center.
Trail Description: The Summit Trail begins to the left of the Visitor
Center. Follow the paved path .25 mile to the top of the mountain
and observation tower. Return the way you came for an easy hike.

BLOWING ROCK:
JULIAN PRICE LAKE TRAIL

Length of Trail: 2.5 miles
Type of Trail: Loop
Condition of Trail: Excellent
Difficulty of Trail: Easy
Approx Hiking Time 1.5-2 hrs
Directions to Trailhead: At mile 297 on the Blue Ridge Parkway,
pull in and park in the parking lot at the lake.
Trail Description: The loop circles the lake. You can walk either way
around the lake from the parking area.

TANAWHA TRAIL

From Wilson Creek Overlook on Blue Ridge Parkway (mile 303.6), to Rough Ridge Parking Area (mile 302.8)
Length of Trail: 1.5 miles one way
Type of Trail: Out and Back, or Loop
Condition of Trail: Rugged
Difficulty of Trail: Moderate to Strenuous
Approx Hiking Time: 2-2.5 hrs roundtrip, depending upon pace
Directions to Trailhead: Start on the Blue Ridge Parkway at mile marker 303.6 at Wilson Creek Overlook.
Trail Description: Walk toward the bridge over Wilson Creek at the north end of the parking lot. The trail starts on the right at that end of the parking lot. Go down the steps and under the Blue Ridge Parkway. The trail meanders over a variety of different habitats and starts climbing to higher elevations with great views. Return the way you came, or walk the Blue Ridge Parkway back for a loop hike.

BOONE:
STONE MOUNTAIN LOOP TRAIL

Length of Trail: 4.7 miles
Type of Trail: Loop
Condition of Trail: Good
Difficulty of Trail: Strenuous
Approx Hiking Time: 4-5 hrs, to take in all the views
Directions to Trailhead: From I-77 North, take Exit 83/hwy 21
North/Sparta/Roaring Gap (Exit from the left lane). Go north about
13 miles to Traphill Road (SR1002). At a brown state park sign, turn
left. Go about 4 miles to John P. Frank Parkway (also a brown state
park sign); turn right. This road brings you into the park. Get a map
at the Visitor Center. Continue approx 3 miles to the lower trailhead
parking area on the John P. Frank Parkway.

Stone Mountain Loop Trail
Continued

Trail Description: From the Trailhead, turn left on the Stone
Mountain Loop Trail. Orange Blazed. At .5 mile, get partial views,
and at 1 mile reach the top of Stone Mountain. At approx 2.5 miles,
reach Stone Mountain Falls. At 3 miles, reach a trail that leads
to the Middle and Lower Falls, and at 3.7 miles, reach a junction of
Cedar and Wolf Rock Trails. At 4 miles, reach the Hutchinson
Homestead. Cross the bridge and continue right, down the road.
Complete the loop soon at 4.7 miles. Take a left to return to the
parking area.

BREVARD:

COURTHOUSE FALLS

Length of Trail: .4 mile one way
Type of Trail: Out and Back
Condition of Trail: Good
Difficulty of Trail: Easy
Approx Hiking Time: 20-30 minutes
Directions to Trailhead: From the Blue Ridge Parkway, go south on hwy 215 for approx 6.5 miles and turn left on FR 140 just after the bridge. From hwy 64, turn north on NC hwy 215. Drive approx 10.3 miles up 215 and turn right on FR 140 just before the bridge. Drive up the gravel road for approx 3 miles and park in the wider area just after the bridge across Courthouse Creek. The trailhead is on the left.
Trail Description: Take the Summey Cove Trail heading downstream beside the creek. At .3 mile take the trail to the left down to the creek and falls. At .4 mile arrive at Courthouse Falls. Return the same way.

DEVIL'S COURTHOUSE TRAIL ON THE BLUE RIDGE PARKWAY

Length of Trail: 1 mile roundtrip
Type of Trail: Out and Back
Condition of Trail: Good. Paved just about the entire length.

Difficulty of Trail: Moderate to strenuous; steep incline.
Approx Hiking Time: 1-1.5 hrs, depending on how long you savor the view.
Directions to Trailhead: Paved parking area on the Blue Ridge Parkway is at MP 422.4
Trail Description: Take the paved trail .5 mile to the observation area at the summit, to amazing views. The Mountains to the Sea Trail comes in from the left at .25 mile.

GRAVEYARD FIELDS
on the Blue Ridge Parkway
Lower or Second Falls

Length of Trail: .3 mile one way
Type of Trail: Out and Back
Condition of Trail: Good
Difficulty of Trail: Easy to Moderate
Approx Hiking Time: 45 Minutes
Directions to Trailhead: Between mile marker 418 and  419 on the Blue Ridge Parkway. At 418.8: Large parking area.
Trail Description: From the parking area, head down the steps heading north on the trail. At .2 mile, cross the bridge over the Yellowstone Prong and take the right trail for approx 125 yards to descend the steps and boardwalks to the base of the falls and a viewing area at .3 mile. After viewing the falls, return the way you came.

HOOKER FALLS DUPONT STATE FOREST

Length of Trail: .4 mile one way
Type of Trail: Out and Back
Condition of Trail: Good
Difficulty of Trail: Easy
Approx. Hiking Time: 30-45 minutes
Directions to Trailhead: Directions from Asheville (via Brevard, NC): Drive I-26 east to exit 40 for hwy280/airport exit toward Brevard. Turn right onto 280 and drive about 16 miles. Turn left on US 64 as you enter Brevard past Wal-Mart. Travel east on US64 for 3.7 miles to the gas station in Penrose. Turn right on Crab Creek Rd and continue 4.3 miles and turn right again on DuPont Road. After 3.1 miles, find the Hooker Falls parking area on the right just before the Little River bridge.
Trail Description: From the Trailhead parking lot, follow the gravel road downstream beside Little River. At .3 mile, come to the observation deck beside the falls. Continue down the road to .4 mile, to reach the beach area across from the falls. Return the way you came.

LOOKING GLASS FALLS

Looking Glass Falls
Length of Trail: Roadside less than 150 feet
Type of Trail: Out and Back
Condition of Trail: Excellent
Difficulty of Trail: Easy
Approx Hiking Time: 5 minutes 1 way
Directions to Trailhead: From the intersection of US 64, US276, and
NC 280 in Brevard, NC take hwy 276 North for 5.5 miles to the
parking area on the right side of the road.
Trail Description: Take the steps down to the base of the falls, less
than 150 feet.

LOOKING GLASS ROCK

Length of Trail: 3.1 miles one way
Type of Trail: Out and Back
Condition of Trail: Good
Difficulty of Trail: Moderate to Strenuous
Approx Hiking Time: 4 hrs
Directions to Trailhead: From the intersection of US hwy 276 /NC
hwy 280 in Brevard, NC, take hwy 276 north for 5.3 miles to FS 475
on the left toward the Pisgah Center for Wildlife Education and Fish
Hatchery. Turn left here and follow FS475 for .4 mile to the
Trailhead on the right.
Trail Description: From the trailhead, hike northwest on the trail.
After about 1 mile, the trail gets a little steeper and starts ascending
some switchbacks. At the 2-mile mark, you will reach an open rock
area with an H on it, used as a Helipad for rescues and training.
Continue to the summit at 3.1 miles for some awesome views.
Return the way you came. Be careful on the rocks during the winter,
especially on ice.

MT. PISGAH, NC

Length of Trail 1.25 miles one way
Type of Trail: Out and Back
Condition of Trail: Good
Difficulty of Trail: Moderate to Strenuous
Approx Hiking Time: 2-3 hrs, depending on how long you enjoy
the view.
Directions to Trailhead: From the Blue Ridge Parkway at milepost
407.6, turn into the Mt Pisgah parking area.
Trail Description: From the parking area at the end of the road, start
hiking behind the trail sign. At .5 mile, the trail gets steeper. At .8
mile and 1 mile there are a couple of benches. At 1.25 miles, arrive
at the tower and observation platform. Enjoy the view.

SHINING ROCK IN THE
SHINING ROCK WILDERNESS

Length of Trail: 10.3 miles roundtrip
Kind of Trail: Loop
Condition of Trail: Mostly good, some areas rutted and rough
Difficulty: Strenuous
Approx.Hiking Time: 5-6 hrs
Directions to Trailhead: From NC hwy 215 and the junction with the Blue Ridge Parkway, head north on the BRP, approx 3 miles, to FS 816 on the left, Black Balsam Rd. Drive to the end of the road, approx 1 mile, to the large parking area and Black Balsam Trailhead.
Trail Description: From the parking area at the end of FS 816, walk back down the road you came in on: Go .5 mile to the Mountains to Sea (MTS)/Art Loeb Trailhead (ALT) on the left. Take the ALT, Section 3, north to Shining Rock Gap at 5.4 miles total. Take the Old Butt Knob Trail (OBKT) .3 miles to the Shining Rock. After seeing the Shining Rock, backtrack to Shining Rock Gap at mile 6. Take the Ivestor Gap Trail south from Shining Rock Gap, 4.3 miles, back to the Black Balsam Parking Area at the end of FS 816 for a roundtrip hike of 10.3 miles. Warning: Make sure you take a map and know how to use it. There are a lot of potentially confusing intersections and unmarked trails in this area.

TRIPLE FALLS AND HIGH FALLS
in Dupont Forest via the Hooker Falls Parking Area

Length of Trail: .5 mile one way to Triple Falls.
1 mile one way to High Falls
Type of Trail: Out and Back
Condition of Trail: Good
Difficulty of Trail: Moderate
Approx Hiking Time: 30 minutes roundtrip to Triple Falls. 1 hr roundtrip to High Falls
Directions to Trailhead: Directions from Asheville (via Brevard): I-26 East to exit 40 for Highway 280/Airport exit toward Brevard. Turn right onto 280 and drive about 16 miles. Turn left on U.S. 64 as you enter Brevard past Wal-Mart. Travel east on U.S. 64 for 3.7 miles to the gas station in Penrose. Turn right on Crab Creek Rd and continue 4.3 miles and turn right again on DuPont Road. After 3.1 miles, find the Hooker Falls parking area on the right just before the Little River Bridge.

Triple Falls
Continued

Trail Description: After parking at the Hooker Falls parking area, climb the stairs at the lower end of the parking lot, to Staton Rd. Cross over the river and to the opposite side of the road, where there is a set of stairs down to the Triple Falls Trail. Take this trail .5 mile to the upper viewing area at Triple Falls. There are also side trails that will take you to the lower part of the falls. To continue to High Falls from the Triple Falls viewing area, continue up the hill and bear left onto the High Falls Trail. At the fork, turn right on the High Falls Trail and continue to the viewing area. Total approx 1 mile. Going left at the fork, the Riverbend Trail will take you to the base of the falls.

BRYSON CITY:
BARTRAM FALLS ON BARTRAM TRAIL

Length of Trail: approx 3 miles one way
Type of Trail: Out and Back
Condition of Trail: Good to Rugged.
Difficulty of Trail: Very Strenuous
Approx Hiking Time: 3.5-4 hrs
Challenge: Take Bartram Trail all the way to the top to Cheoah Bald
Length of Trail: 5.1 miles one way
Type of Trail: Out and Back
Condition of Trail: Rugged
Difficulty of Trail: Very Difficult
Approx Hiking Time: 6-7 hrs
Elevation Gain: 3,000 ft
Directions to Trailhead: Winding Stairs Parking Area: From the intersection of Wayah Road and US hwy 19/74. Travel US hwy 19/74 northeast, approx 1.1 miles to FS 422 on the right. Take FS 422 and the Winding Stairs Parking Area is immediately on the right at the bulletin board.
Trail Description: Walk back down FS 422 toward the highway and cross over the highway. Be careful! A lot of traffic on this highway. Cross over the railroad tracks and begin following the trail to the left, parallel to the highway and the river. The trail will then start switchbacks heading up the mountain to reach Bartram Falls at approx 3 miles. Cheoah Bald at 5.1 miles. Intersects the AT at 4.9 miles. Take a right on the AT and follow the Bartram .2 miles to Cheoah Bald. Note: The Bartram Trail and the AT run together the last .2 miles to Cheoah Bald.

DEEP CREEK LOOP IN THE SMOKIES

Length of Trail:
4.4 miles

Type of Trail: Loop
Condition of trail: Good
Difficulty of Trail: Moderate
Approx Hiking Time: 2-3 hrs
Directions to Trailhead: From downtown Bryson City, follow Deep Creek Rd approx 3 miles to the end of the road. Pass the campground to the parking area and take the Deep Creek Trail, which parallels Deep Creek on the left side.
Trail Description: Take the Deep Creek Trail on the old road bed north. At .25 mile, pass Tom Branch Falls, continuing on the Deep Creek Trail for .7 mile, from the trailhead to the beginning of the Deep Creek/Indian Creek Loop. DO NOT take the Indian Creek Trail to the right. You will come back down this trail later to complete the loop. Stay left on the Deep Creek Trail and head north another 1 mile. Look for the marker for the loop trail onto which you turn right, about a dozen feet beyond a bridge over which you cross, to the right of the creek. Follow the loop trail 1.2 miles over Sunkota Ridge to the Indian Creek Trail. At approx .6 mile on the loop trail, you will pass the Sunkota Ridge Trail heading north. Continue past this intersection on the loop trail another .6 mile to reach the Indian Creek Trail. Take a right on the Indian Creek Trail and follow it back to the beginning of the loop .8 mile passing Indian Creek Falls. Take a left on the Deep Creek Trail to return to the trailhead.

CASHIERS:
PANTHERTOWN VALLEY, NC

Length of Trail: 6.6 miles
Type of trail: Loop
Condition of Trail: Good. Rough in some spots.
Difficulty of Trail: Moderate
Approx Hiking Time: 4-5 hrs, depending on how long you enjoy the views.
Directions to Trailhead: From Highlands, NC take US 64 East to Cashiers, NC. Two miles past the stoplight, turn left on Cedar Creek Rd. Go 2.3 miles and turn right on Breedlove Road. The parking area is at the end of the road in just under 4 miles. The last part of this road may be rough.
Trail Description: From the Salt Rock trailhead, follow the gravel road down into the valley. At .2 miles take a right on the Wilderness Falls Trail, passing the falls. Continue until the intersection with the Deep Gap Trail at 1.1 miles. A spur trail goes down to Frolic Town Falls. Take a left on the Deep Gap Trail and continue to the intersection of the Great Wall Trail at 1.2 miles. Take a right on the Great Wall Trail, and continue to approx 1.5 miles. Take a left on the

Panthertown Valley, NC
Continued

Granny Burrell Falls Trail, passing Granny Burrell Falls at 1.7 miles and continue to the intersection with Mac's Gap Trail at 1.9 miles. Take a right on Mac's Gap Trail, continuing along the valley floor, passing the Green Valley Trail at 2.7 miles to Little Green Mt. Trail at 2.9 miles.

Take a left on Little Green Mountain Trail, which starts as a moderate climb, but gets steep, climbing a series of steps up the side of Little Green. Once on the top, the trail follows the contour of the ridge line, and one must navigate across barren rock. The trail can be a little difficult to follow. Watch for faint white arrows painted on the rocks' surfaces and occasionally a green marker nailed to a tree or an exposed root. There are some tremendous views of the valley along this stretch. After viewing Tranquility Point, follow the steep trail down the backside of the mountain to School House Falls at 3.9 miles. From the falls back track a little distance and head north on the trail to reach Panthertown Valley Trail at approx 4.1 miles. Turn left on the Panthertown Valley Trail and follow the trail back to Salt Rock trailhead completing a loop of approx 6.6 miles.

SILVER RUN FALLS, CASHIERS, NC

Length of Trail: .2 mile one way
Type of Trail: Out and Back
Condition of Trail: Good
Difficulty of Trail: Easy
Approx Hiking Time: 15 minutes
Directions to Trailhead: From the intersection of US hwy 64/NC
hwy 107, take hwy 107 south for 4 miles to a gravel parking area on
the left side of the road.
Trail Description: From the parking area, head back into the woods.
At about the half way point, cross over a footbridge and continue on
to the falls at approx .2 mile.

WHITESIDE MOUNTAIN

Length of Trail: 2 miles
Type of Trail: Loop
Condition of Trail: Good
Difficulty of Trail: Moderate
Approx Hiking Time: 2-2.5 hrs
Directions to Trailhead: From Highlands, NC, take US 64 east approx 5.5 miles. Turn right at the sign for Whiteside Mountain Recreation Area and Whiteside Mt. Rd. Follow this road 1 mile to the signed parking area on the left. There is a day area-use fee at Whiteside Mountain Recreation Area.
Trail Description: From the parking area, head up the mountain trail behind the trail sign. At .1 mile, reach the loop part of the trail. To the left, follow an old logging road all the way to the top, approx 1 mile. To the right, climb the stairs, and reach the viewpoints for the cliffs the further you climb. The loop is 2 miles.

CHEROKEE:
FLAT CREEK TRAIL

Length of Trail: 6.2 miles for Loop. 5.2 miles for Out and Back
Type of Trail: Loop or Out and Back
Condition of Trail: Good
Difficulty of Trail: Moderate
Approx Hiking Time: 3.5-4 hrs
Directions to Trailhead: The trailhead begins at the end of Heintooga
Ridge Rd before it turns into Balsam Mt Rd (gated in the winter),
located at milepost 458 on the Blue Ridge Parkway. At milepost
458, turn onto Heintooga Ridge Rd, and follow it to the turnaround
at approx 8.8 miles, to the picnic area. The trail starts to the right of
the picnic area.
Trail Description: From the trailhead it is .1 mile to Heintooga
Overlook. Take in the long range views and continue through the
open forest to a spur trail to Flat Creek Falls at 1.9 miles. [Because
of limited views, I did not include the hike to Flat Creek Falls.]
Continuing past the spur trail, reach the end of the trail at Heintooga
Ridge Rd at 2.6 miles. To make this a loop hike, you can take a left
and walk down the road 3.6 miles back to the picnic area you started
from, giving you a total of 6.2 miles. Or turn around and backtrack
on the Flat Creek Trail for an out-and-back of 5.2 miles.

MINGO FALLS CHEROKEE, NC

Length of Trail: .2 mile one way
Type of Trail: Out and Back
Condition of Trail: Good
Difficulty of Trail: Easy to Moderate
Approx Hiking Time: 20-30 minutes roundtrip
Directions to Trailhead: From the intersection of hwy 441/19, drive
north on hwy 441 for approx 2.2 miles and take a right on Acquoni
Rd for .1 mile and then take a left on Big Cove Rd for approx 4.7
miles, passing the KOA Campground on the right. Turn right at the
Mingo Falls sign onto Mingo Falls Bridge Rd, and go over the
bridge to the parking area.
Trail Description: From the parking area, walk up a set of about 150
steps. The trail then levels and follows the creek upstream to an
observation area and footbridge at approx .2 mile. An easy return.

CHIMNEY ROCK:
CHIMNEY ROCK

Length of Trail: Rocky Broad River Walk: .25 miles roundtrip
Skyline Trail: .7 miles roundtrip
Type of Trail: Out and Back
Condition of Trail: Good
Difficulty of Trail: Rocky Broad River Walk: Easy
The Skyline Trail: Moderate
Approx Hiking Time: Rocky Broad River Walk: 15 minutes
The Skyline Trail: 45 minutes
Directions to Trailhead: From Asheville, NC, take Interstate 26 East
toward Hendersonville to Exit # 49A (Bat Cave and Highway 64
East). Stay on 64 East for 18 miles and the park entrance will be on
the right. Get a map at the park entrance. Rocky Broad River Walk is
at the park entrance. The Skyline Trail starts near the actual
Chimney Rock, close to the gift shop.
Trail Description: The Rocky Broad River Walk goes .25 mile,
round trip, beside the river with huge boulders near the park
entrance. The Skyline Trail climbs about 150 feet to the highest
lookout in the park, Exclamation Point.

FRANKLIN:
ALBERT MOUNTAIN Access (Bypass) Trail, NC

Length of Trail: .5 mile one way
Type of Trail: Out and Back
Condition of Trail: Good
Difficulty of Trail: Moderate
Approx. Hiking Time: 1 hrs
Directions to Trailhead: From the Intersection of hwy 441/ hwy 64
near Franklin, NC Take hwy 64 west for 11.8 miles and take a left
onto West Old Murphy Rd /Wallace Gap Rd/ SR1448 at the sign for
Wallace Gap/Standing Indian Campground. Drive 1.8 miles to
Wallace Gap and take a right on FS 67. Go 9.7 miles on FS67
(staying left at the fork at mile 1.7. The right fork goes to the
campground. turns to gravel at mile 2.2 and could be gated in the
winter) to the intersection of FS 67 and FS 83. From this
intersection of FS 67 and FS 83 (towards Coweeta Hydrologic
Laboratory and Pickens Nose Trail) bear left, staying on FS 67 for
another 2.1 miles to the end of road. Total of 11.8 miles on FS 67.
Trail Description: From the parking area there are no signs for
Albert Mountain Fire Tower, only a gated jeep trail at the back of the
parking area. Take this trail for about .3 mile until you intersect
the (White Blazed) Appalachian Trail. Take a right onto the AT and
continue up the ridge (steep incline) about .2 mile to the top of
Albert Mountain to the fire tower and an awesome view.

BEECH CREEK LOOP TRAIL INCLUDING HIGH FALLS in the SOUTHERN NANTAHALA WILDERNESS

Length of Trail: 8 miles
Type of Trail: Loop
Condition of Trail: Good. Rough in a few spots.
Difficulty of Trail: Strenuous
Approx Hiking Time: 5-6 hrs
Directions to Trailhead: From Clayton, GA take US 76 West for 8 miles to Persimmon Rd on the right. Take Persimmon Rd 4.2 miles to Tallulah River Rd on the left. Take Tallulah River Rd for approx 9 miles to the end to a parking area/turn around and Northern Trailhead.
Trail Description: Take the old road that continues straight behind the bulletin board and road-blocking boulders. Continue on to reach the intersection with the Deep Gap Trail at .4 miles on the left. Continue straight on the Beech Creek Trail climbing steadily to reach the ridge at 1.6 miles. Continue climbing to reach Case Knife Gap at 3 miles. From the Gap continue southeast reaching a sharp turn to the right and side path to the left to High Falls at 4.5 miles. It is .1 mile to High Falls and well worth the effort. After visiting the falls backtrack back to the trail and continue downhill coming out beside Beech Creek at 4.8 miles. Continue downhill to reach the first crossing of Beech Creek at 5.9 miles and another crossing at 6.6 miles. You will reach Tallulah River Rd at 6.8 miles. Take a right on Tallulah River Rd, heading north for another 1.2 miles to reach the Northern Trailhead and parking area completing an 8-mile loop.

PICKENS NOSE TRAIL, NC

Pickens Nose Trail, NC
Continued

Length of Trail: .7 mile one way
Type of Trail: Out and Back
Condition of Trail: Good
Difficulty of Trail: Moderate
Approx Hiking time: 1 hr
Directions to Trailhead: From the intersection of US 441/ Coweeta
Lab Rd near Otto, NC. Take Coweeta Lab Rd / FS 83 (Ball Creek
Rd) approx 9 miles to the trailhead on the left side of FS 83.
Trail Description: From the trailhead take the Pickens Nose Trail,
climbing steadily up through the rhododendron-lined path. At about
the halfway point, the views open up to the left, off the side of the
mountain. Continue to a great view at the end of the trail at .7 mile.
Return the way you came.

SILER BALD NEAR FRANKLIN, NC

Length of Trail: 1.8 miles one way. 3.6 miles roundtrip
Type of Trail: Out and Back
Condition of Trail: Good
Difficulty of Trail: Moderate
Approx Hiking Time: 2-3 hrs
Directions to Trailhead: From the intersection of hwy 441/hwy 64 in
Franklin, NC take hwy 64 West for 3.8 miles to Old Murphy Rd
(SR1448) on the right. Go .1 mile to Wayah Rd (SR 1310) on the
Left. Go 9 miles to Wayah Gap. Now, look to the left and you'll see
a road on your left as you just pass FS 69. Take this road for about
0.2 miles to "Wayah Crest" Picnic Area.
Trail Description: Pick up the White Blazed "Appalachian Trail"
here. Take the AT south for 1.6 miles to a clearing. From here you
can catch a glimpse of the open summit of Siler Bald on the right.
Climb the open meadow on a well-worn path .2 mile for a view of
the surrounding mountains. Do not confuse with Siler's Bald in the
Smokies.

STANDING INDIAN MOUNTAIN, NC

Length of Trail: 2.5 Miles One Way
Type of Trail: Out and Back
Condition of Trail: Good
Difficulty of Trail: Moderate
Approx Hiking Time: 3-4 hrs
Directions to Trailhead: From the Intersection US hwy 441/64 in
Franklin, NC, Take hwy 64 west for 14.5 miles to FS 71 on the left
just past the Macon/Clay county line. Take FS 71, and go 5.9 miles
to the end at Deep Gap.
Trail Description: Take the AT (Appalachian Trail) north 2.5 miles
from Deep Gap to the top of Standing Indian Mountain.
Return the way you came.

BIG LAUREL FALLS

Length of Trail: .6 mile one way, 1.2 miles roundtrip.
Type of Trail: Out and Back
Condition of Trail: Good
Difficulty of Trail: Easy to Moderate
Approx. Hiking Time: 30-45 minutes
Directions to Trailhead: From the Intersection of hwy 441/hwy 64
Take hwy 64 west for 11.8 miles and take a left onto West Old
Murphy Rd /Wallace Gap Rd. SR 1448 at the sign for Wallace Gap/
Standing Indian Campground, and drive 1.8 miles to Wallace Gap
and take a right on FS67. Go 1.7 miles on FS67, staying left at the
fork. (Right fork goes to campground.) Road turns to gravel and
could be gated in winter. Continue another 5 miles to trailhead on
the right for Laurel Falls Trail and Timber Ridge Trail.
Trail Description: From the Trailhead, after walking a few feet, turn
right to stay on Laurel Falls Trail. After about 75 yards, cross a
footbridge over Mooney Creek. Immediately after crossing the
bridge, you come to a T intersection. Timber Ridge Trail goes left.
Take a right and follow Mooney Creek downstream on the Laurel
Falls Trail. After the trail goes away from Mooney Creek, it follows
Kilby Creek upstream past the intersection of Big Laurel Branch to
the falls. Return the way you came.

WAYAH BALD SUMMIT TRAIL

Length of Trail: .1 mile roundtrip
Type of Trail: Out and Back
Condition of Trail: Excellent. Paved.
Difficulty of Trail: Easy
Approx Hiking Time: 10 minutes
Directions to Trailhead: From the Intersection of hwy 441/64 in
Franklin, NC. Take hwy 64 West for 3.8 miles to Old Murphy Rd.
(SR 1448) on the right. Go 1 mile to Wayah Rd (SR 1310) on the
left. Go 9 miles to Wayah Gap. Take a right on FS 69 for 4.3 miles
to the end at Wayah Bald.
Trail Description: Take the paved path less than .1 mile to the
observation tower.

HIGHLANDS:
BARTRAM TRAIL
Jones Gap to Jones Knob and Whiterock Mountain

Length of Trail: 2.6 miles one way
Type of Trail: Out and Back
Condition of Trail: Good
Difficulty: Moderate
Approx Hiking Time: 3-3.5 hrs
Directions to Trailhead: Driving distance/direction from downtown Highlands, NC: Follow hwy 64 west 4.6 miles. Watch for the Cliffside Lake entrance on the right. Just past Cliffside Lake, turn left on Turtle Pond Road. Follow Turtle Pond Road for 1.1 miles to Dendy Orchard Road. Turn right on Dendy Orchard Road and follow it for 1.4 miles. This will become a steep dirt road. At the top of the hill, turn left onto Jones Gap Road. A Bartram Trail sign indicates this road. Follow it 2 miles to a parking area at the top of the gap.
Trail Description: From the parking area, follow an old roadbed through a wildlife clearing, to reach the intersection of Jones Knob Trail at .3 mile. Take the Jones Knob Trail .3 mile to a great view and back, adding .6 mile to the hike. Well worth the effort. From here head north on the Bartram Trail, and at 1.7 miles, reach a spur trail to a view of White Rock Mt. At 1.9 miles, reach White Rock Gap. Continue on to mile 2.4 to a spur trail to the left and to White Rock Mt. Follow this trail approx .2 mile to White Rock Mountain with great views of the surrounding mountains at mile 2.6 total. Return the way you came.

CHATTOOGA RIVER LOOP
Trail at Bull Pen Bridge

Length of Trail: 2 miles roundtrip
Type of Trail: Loop
Condition: Good
Difficulty of Trail: Moderate
Approx Hiking Time: 1.5 hrs
Directions to Trailhead: From downtown Highlands, NC, take Main Street east, which turns into Horse Cove Rd for approx 4.5 miles to a fork. To the left is Whiteside Cove Rd, and to the right is Bull Pen Rd. Take a right on Bull Pen Rd, and travel 3 miles to the Bull Pen "Iron Bridge."
Trail Description: The trailhead for the Loop starts at the Bull Pen Bridge, the "Iron Bridge," and proceeds upriver for about a mile. There will be a sign before switching back to the left, and returning through the forest to a campsite, slightly before the parking lot on Bull Pen Road, totaling about 2 miles roundtrip. If you continue to the right at the loop part of the hike, you will be on the Chattooga River Cliffs Trail, a much longer trail.

CLIFFSIDE LOOP

Length of Trail: .75 mile
Type of Trail: Loop
Condition of Trail: Excellent
Difficulty of Trail: Easy
Approx Hiking Time: 30 minutes
Directions to Trailhead: From Downtown Highlands drive west on
US 64 for approx 4.4 miles to Cliffside Lakes Recreation area on the
right. Drive to the end of the road with parking near the lake.
Trail Description: Easy Pleasant Trail that loops around the lake.

DRY FALLS

Length of Trail: Approx 100 yards down some steps.
Type of Trail: Out and Back
Condition of Trail: Paved
Difficulty of Trail: Easy

Dry Falls Continued

Photo taken in the cave behind the waterfall.

Approx Hiking Time: 15 minutes
Directions to Trailhead: From Highlands, drive west on US64 for 3.3 miles. Look for Dry Falls sign and parking area on the left.
Trail Description: paved roadside trail.

Dry Falls is featured in a Silver Angel Award winning kid's show produced in Spartanburg, SC. See Dry Falls on:
YouTube – BehindTheWaterfallTVShow.

GLEN FALLS IN HIGHLANDS, NC.

Length of Trail: 1 mile one way
Type of Trail: Out and Back
Condition of Trail: Good in some places. Rough in other places.
Difficulty of Trail: Strenuous
Approx Hiking Time 1-1.5 hrs
Directions to Trailhead: From the intersection of US hwy 64 /NC hwy 106 in Highlands, NC, take hwy 106 south for 1.8 miles, and take a left at Glen Falls Rd/ SR 1618, and then immediately take a right and follow Glen Falls Rd 1 mile to the parking area.
Trail Description: From the parking area, take the Glen Falls Trail approx .25 mile to a trail that leads to the viewing area for the upper falls. At .4 mile, reach the base of the upper falls. Continue to .8 mile, to reach the base of the middle falls, and another .2 mile, reaching the lower falls at 1 mile. Return the way you came.

HIGHLANDS BOTANICAL GARDENS

Length of Trail: 1 mile total
Nature Center Trail: .1 mile
Woodland Loop: .1 mile
Foreman Loop: .1 mile
Falls Trail: .1 mile
Fern Trail: .1 mile
Lower Lake Trail: .1 mile
Upper Lake Trail: .2 mile
Coker Rhododendron Trail .2 mile
Type of Trails: Loop and Out and Back
Condition of Trail: Good
Difficulty of Trail: Easy
Approx Hiking Time: 1 hr
Direction to Trailhead: From Highlands, NC, go east on Main St, which turns into Horse Cove Rd, about .5 mile to the Nature Center, and park across the street.
Trail Description: Obtain Trail Map at the Nature Center. Take the Nature Center Trail behind the Nature Center and Amphitheater to reach the other trails.

SCALY MOUNTAIN, NC via Bartram Trail

Length of Trail: 1.9 miles one way

Type of Trail: Out and Back
Condition of Trail: Good
Difficulty of Trail: Moderate
Approx Hiking Time: 2-3 hrs
Directions to the Trailhead: From downtown Highlands, NC, take hwy 106 south, approx 5.5 miles to the Osage Mountain Overlook. Park at the overlook. The trail starts up the mountain on the opposite side of the hwy.
Directions to alternate trailhead on Hickory Knut Road (SR 1621): From Highlands, NC, take hwy 106 south for approx 4 miles. Turn right on Turtle Pond Road. Drive .25 mile and turn left on to Hickory Knut Rd. Drive .9 mile to the top of the Gap. The trail, a Forest Service Rd, is on the left. Park on the right side of the road. Walk up the road and, at .28 mile, the trail leaves the road to the right. Follow the Blue Blazed Trail to the junction with the Bartram Trail and take a right on the Bartram Trail.
Trail Description: Across the hwy from the Osage Mountain Overlook, take the Bartram Trail north up the mountain. At .3 mile, take a side trail to a waterfall. At .9 mile, turn right on the roadbed. At 1.4 miles, you will reach an access trail to the right that leads to Hickory Knut Road. Bartram Trail bears to the left. At 1.9 miles, reach the top of Scaly Mountain with great views.

SUNSET ROCK TRAIL

Length of Trail: .5 mile one way
Type of Trail: Out and Back.
Condition of Trail: Excellent
Difficulty of Trail: Easy
Approx Hiking Time: 30-45 minutes, depending on how long you take in the views.
Direction to Trailhead: From Highlands, NC, go east on Main St, which turns into Horse Cove Rd, about .5 mile to the Nature Center, and park across the street.
Trail Description: From the parking area, follow the gravel roadbed up to the top of the mountain to Sunset Rock on the right. Also there is another view on the left near the turnaround. It is possible to drive a car up, but much more fun to walk up and enjoy nature.

HOT SPRINGS:

LOVER'S LEAP

Length of Trail: 1.6 miles
Type of Trail: Loop;
Condition of Trail: Good
Difficulty of Trail: Moderate due to steepness getting to the ridge
Approx Hiking Time: 1.5-2 hrs

Directions to the Trailhead: From the parking areas in downtown Hot Springs near the railroad tracks (on Andrews Ave. N or Andrews Ave. S), walk east on hwy 25/70 past the Hot Springs Spa and walk over the bridge, following the AT markers. At the eastern end of the bridge, climb over the guard rail, down a set of stairs to the street below, by the French Broad River. Continue on Silvermine Rd, following AT markers, past the Nantahala Outdoor Center. The AT starts where Silvermine Creek Rd swings left. This is where you return to close the loop. Continue right, following the AT north along the river.

Trail Description: From the point where Silvermine Creek Rd goes left and the AT starts straight ahead, go north following the river. Go approx 1.3 miles north on the AT, along the river at first, and then heading up the mountain, where it starts getting steep, for several good viewpoints of the river and the town of Hot Springs. Continue on the AT to the cut off for the Lovers Leap Trail/Silvermine Trail to the left. Take this trail .3 mile, back to the Silvermine Creek Rd parking area, and continue, back down the road to the point you started the loop. From this point go back to downtown the way you came.

LINVILLE:

ELK RIVER FALLS

Length of Trail: .2 mile one way
Condition of Trail: Good
Difficulty of Trail: Easy
Approx Hiking Time: 20 minutes roundtrip
Directions to Trailhead: From the TN/NC state line on US hwy19,
go east approx 1 mile as you are coming into the town of Elk Park.

Take a left at the sign for Elk River Falls on Old Mill Rd. Go approx 1/4 of a mile on Old Mill Rd. Take a left on Elk River Rd, and go approx 4 miles to the end at the parking area.
Trail Description: Follow the trail, going downstream on the Elk River .2 mile to the falls. There is viewing at the top of the falls and a wide area at the base.

HAWK'S BILL MOUNTAIN - LINVILLE GORGE

Length of Trail: Approx 2 miles roundtrip
Type of Trail: Out and Back
Condition of Trail: Good at the beginning. Rugged near the top
Difficulty of the Trail: Moderate to Strenuous, due to steepness of trail.
Approx Hiking Time: 1.5-2 hrs, depending upon how long you enjoy
the view.
Directions to the Trailhead: From the intersection of NC hwy 181/183,
travel south approx 2 miles to NC 1265, Ginger Cake Rd, on the right.
Go approx 2.5 miles to NC 1264 on the right, with a sign to Table
Rock. Take NC 1264 approx another mile, where it turns to gravel at
approx 3.5 miles. Go approx 1.5 miles after the road turns to gravel; it's
about 5 miles to the Sitting Bear Trailhead on the right.
Trail Description: From The Sitting Bear Trailhead, head straight up the
hill. After about .1 mile, you will come to a campsite on the ridge crest
and T intersection with the Jonas Ridge Trail. Take a left here and
follow the Jonas Ridge Trail about .7 mile to the Hawks Bill Trail. At
the intersection with the Hawks Bill Trail, there may or may not be a
sign or post. Go left for a short distance, and then bear right to reach the
summit in another .2 mile. Return the way you came.

LINVILLE FALLS – ERWIN'S VIEW

Length of Trail: 1.8 miles roundtrip
Type of Trail: Out and Back
Condition of Trail: Good
Difficulty of Trail: Easy for Upper Falls. Moderate for Chimney View and Erwin's View
Approx Hiking Time: 1-1.5 hrs
Directions to the Trailhead: From mile marker 316.4 on the Blue Ridge Parkway, follow the Linville Falls Spur Rd to the Visitor Center and park in the large parking lot.
Trail Description: Starting from behind the Visitor's Center, follow the paved trail over the bridge. The trail then turns to gravel and then to dirt the further you go out. Upper Falls is about .5 mile, Chimney View .7 mile, and Erwin's View .9 mile.

ROAN HIGH BLUFF

Length of Trail: 1 mile for both loops at the Rhododendron Gardens; .5 mile one way to the viewing platform at Roan High Bluff.
Type of Trail: 2 loops at the Rhododendron Gardens, and an Out and Back to Roan High Bluff.
Condition of Trail: Excellent for the Rhododendron Gardens. Good for Roan High Bluff.
Difficulty of Trail: Easy for the Rhododendron Gardens and Easy to Moderate for Roan High Bluff.
Approx Hiking Time: 1.5-2 hrs total for both.
Direction to the Trailhead: From Roan Mountain, TN, take hwy 143 south for approx 13 miles to the top of the mountain at Carver's Gap at the TN/NC state line. Take the access road to the Rhododendron Gardens and go a little over a mile to the Visitor Center for the gardens and on down the gravel road around the bus parking loop for the trailhead to Roan High Bluff on the right.

Trail Description: For Rhododendron Gardens: From the information building and restrooms, take the paved trail to the upper loop. This loop has interpretive information at different stops. Also, take the lower loop, which is gravel/natural surface to great views of the rhododendron.

Trail Description: For Roan High Bluff: From the trailhead on the gravel road, take the trail .5 mile to the viewing platform for magnificent views.

ROAN HIGH GARDENS

PLUNGE BASIN OVERLOOK, LINVILLE GORGE
TRAIL (Blue Ridge Parkway)

Length of Trail: Plunge Basin Overlook Trail: .5 mile one way.
Linville Gorge Trail: .8 mile one way
Type of Trail: Out and Back
Condition of Trail: Good
Difficulty of Trail: PBO: Moderate
                    LGT: Moderate to Strenuous
Approx Hiking Time: for both trails: 2-3 hrs, depending on how long
you enjoy the view.
Directions to Trailhead: From mile marker 316.4 on the Blue Ridge
Parkway, follow the Linville Falls Spur Rd to the Visitor Center and
park in the large parking lot.
Trail Description: The two trails start to the right of the Visitor
Center and share the same path for the first .3 mile. At .3 mile, the
PBO Trail continues straight for another .2 mile to the overlook. The
LGT goes to the left and continues another .5 mile to the base of
Linville Falls.

SALUDA:

PEARSON'S FALLS, NC

Length of Trail: .3 mile one way
Type of Trail: Out and Back
Condition of Trail: Excellent
Difficulty of Trail: Easy
Approx Hiking Time: 30-45 minutes
Direction to Trailhead: From I-26, Exit 59, drive SW on Ozone Dr/ SR 1142, toward Saluda, NC, for 1.1 mile, where it dead ends into US hwy 176. Take a left on hwy 176 and drive 2.5 miles to Pearson's Falls Rd on the right. Take Pearson's Falls Rd a little less than a mile, to the entrance. Pay the fee and continue to the parking area.
Trail Description: From the parking area, follow the trail alongside the creek .3 mile to the base of the falls. After viewing the falls, return the way you came for a roundtrip hike of .6 mile.

SAPHIRE:
RAINBOW, TURTLE BACK, AND DRIFT FALLS
On the Horse Pasture River

RAINBOW

**TURTLE
BACK**

Length of Trail: Rainbow Falls 1.5 miles, Turtleback Falls 1.7 miles, Drift Falls 1.8 miles, all one way.
Type of Trail: Out and Back
Condition of Trail: Good

Rainbow, Turtle Back, and Drift Falls
on the Horsepasture River
Continued:

Difficulty of Trail: Moderate
Approx Hiking Time 2.5-3 hrs
Direction to Trailhead: From the intersection of US hwy 64 and NC 281 in Sapphire, NC, drive south on 281 for .7 mile to the Grassy Ridge access area on the left (west side of the park). From the entrance, follow the park loop road, approx 1.5 miles, bearing right, past the visitor center to the large parking area for the falls on the Horsepasture River.

DRIFT FALLS

Trail Description: From the parking area and information board, take the Rainbow Falls Trail, exiting the park at a little less than a mile to National Forest Land, where the trail gets a little less well-maintained. In another .25 mile, you will be walking beside Horsepasture River. Head upstream. At this point you have another .4 mile to go and the final .25 mile gets steeper as you approach Rainbow Falls at 1.5 miles. To reach Turtleback Falls, continue in the same direction another .2 mile, at 1.7 miles. Drift Falls is another .1 in the same direction at 1.8 miles. Return the way you came.

WHITEWATER FALLS AND LAUREL FALLS ON CORBIN CREEK

Length of Trail: 1 mile one way
Type of Trail: Out and Back
Condition of Trail: Good
Difficulty of Trail: Moderate
Approx Hiking Time: 1.5-2 hrs
Directions to Trailhead: Drive approx 8.5 miles south on hwy 281 from the intersection of hwy 64/281 in Sapphire, NC. Look for the sign for the left turn into the parking area. There is a parking fee.
Trail Description: From the parking area, head uphill on the paved path, approx .25 mile to the end of the paved path and upper viewing deck. From the upper viewing area, take the set of stairs down to the lower viewing deck. From the lower viewing deck, continue down the steps. At approx .5 mile, continuing down the steps, bear left at the fork to continue to the river. At .8 mile, cross the bridge over the Whitewater River and head downstream. At this point there are huge boulders in the river. In another .2 mile, reach Laurel (Corbin Creek) Falls at 1 mile. Backtrack the way you came to the parking area for a 2-mile roundtrip hike.

SYLVA:
RICHLAND BALSAM MOUNTAIN

Length of Trail: 1.4 miles
Type of Trail: Loop
Difficulty of Trail: Moderate
Condition of Trail: Good, Rough in some Places
Approx Hiking Time: 45 minutes -1 hr
Directions to Trailhead: Located at mile marker 431 on the Blue
Ridge Parkway at the Haywood-Jackson Overlook.
Trail Description: Starts off paved. After about .1 mile, reach the
loop section of the hike. You can walk either direction. Described
here, take a right and go counter-clockwise. Reach a bench at the
summit elevation, 6410 feet, at .6 mile. At 1.1 miles, reach another
bench with a good view. At 1.4 miles return to the trailhead.

THE PINNACLE

Length of Trail: 3.3 miles one way
Type of Trail: Out and Back
Condition of Trail: Generally Good. Rough in some places.
Difficulty of Trail: Very Strenuous.
Approx Hiking Time: 4-5 hrs
Directions to Trailhead: From Main St. in Sylva, NC, drive southeast
a little less than a mile to the intersection of Bus Hwy 23 and NC
hwy 107. Take a left on Bus 23 and drive .2 mile and take a left on
Skyland Drive (SR 1432). Drive 1.7 miles on Skyland Drive and
take a left on Fisher Creek Rd. Drive to the end of Fisher Creek Rd,
a little over 2 miles to the parking area.
Trail Description: Follow the West Fork Trail behind the metal gate
on an old roadbed. At .4 miles, reach the intersection of West Fork
and East Fork Trail. Stay left on the West Fork Trail. At 2.0 miles
reach the intersection of the Pinnacle Trail and Black Rock Trail.
Stay left on the Pinnacle Trail. Sign indicates another 1.4 miles.
Keep walking through Rhododendron and keep bearing left to pop
out on the Pinnacle at 3.3 miles. Return the way you came.

WATERROCK KNOB

BLUE RIDGE PARKWAY
WATERROCK KNOB TRAIL

WATERROCK KNOB TRAIL
BLUE RIDGE PARKWAY

Length of Trail: .5 mile one way
Type of Trail: Out and Back
Condition of Trail: Good. Starts out paved but becomes more undefined the further you go up.
Difficulty of Trail: Moderate to Strenuous near the top.
Approx Hiking Time: 30-45 minutes.
Directions to Trailhead: At milepost 451.2 on The Blue Ridge Parkway, take the entrance road to the parking lot at the Visitor Center.
Trail Description: The trail starts at the parking lot near the Visitor Center. At .2 mile is a paved observation area. At .5 miles reach the end of the Trail. Limited views. Return the way you came.

WAYNESVILLE:
BIG CREEK TRAIL TO THE BRIDGE
PAST MOUSE CREEK FALLS

Length of Trail: 2.4 miles one way
Type of Trail: Out and Back
Condition of Trail: Good
Difficulty of Trail: Easy to Midnight Hole. Moderate to the bridge and turn-around point.
Approx Hiking Time: 2.5 hrs
Directions to Trailhead: On I-40 in TN near the TN/NC state line, take Exit 451. Cross the Pigeon River. Turn left at the end of the bridge and follow the road upstream to the Carolina Power and Light Company. Follow the road past the power plant approx 2 miles from the interstate. Continue straight through the intersection to a narrow road to the ranger station for about .2 mile. Continue past the ranger station about .7 mile to the picnic area and campground. Sometimes the road is closed during winter; if so, add another 1.4 mile roundtrip of walking from the ranger station.
Trail Description: From the parking area, take the wide-gated old logging roadbed that parallels Big Creek. At approx 1.5 miles, reach Midnight Hole. With huge boulders and pockets of deep water, carefully continue to 2.2 miles from the parking area to view Mouse Creek Falls. At 2.4 miles, the trail crosses a bridge over Big Creek. This is the turnaround point for this hike. Return the way you came.

BOOGERMAN TRAIL IN THE SMOKIES

Length of Trail: 7.5 miles
Type of Trail: Loop
Condition of Trail: Good
Difficulty of Trail: Moderate
Approx Hiking Time: 4-5 hrs
Directions to Trailhead: From I-40, take Exit 20 (hwy 276). Take the first right onto Cove Creek Rd. Drive approx 6 miles to Cove Creek Gap at the park entrance, and head down into the Catalochee Valley. At the 4-way intersection, turn left and go approx 3.5 miles to the trailhead. The trailhead is a few hundred yards on the left, past campground on Catalochee Road. Park on right, past the Caldwell Fork Trailhead on left. Walk back to trailhead.
Trail Description: Start by crossing Catalochee Creek on a long log foot bridge on the Caldwell Fork Trail. Reach first intersection with Boogerman Trail at .8 mile. You can continue straight on the Caldwell Fork Trail to the other end of Boogerman Trail, or take a left and walk the loop clockwise.

MOUNT STERLING TRAIL

Length of Trail: 2.7 miles one way
Condition of Trail: Good to rugged, the higher you go.
Difficulty of Trail: Strenuous
Approx Hiking Time 4-5 hrs
Directions to Trailhead: Exit 451 on I-40. Cross over the Pigeon
River and turn left at the end of the
bridge on SR 1332. Drive approx 2
miles to 4-way intersection. Turn left
onto NC 284, and go 6.7 miles on a
narrow winding road, to reach Mount
Sterling Gap, on the right side of the
road. Trail begins behind the gated road.
Trail Description: Follow the roadbed
behind the gate, for 2.3 miles to the top
of the ridge. Take a right on Mt Sterling
Ridge Trail and go .4 mile past campsite
38 to Mt. Sterling Firetower.

SOUTH CAROLINA

Hiking Trails

Overview

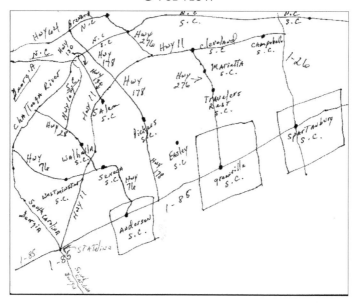

Western South Carolina

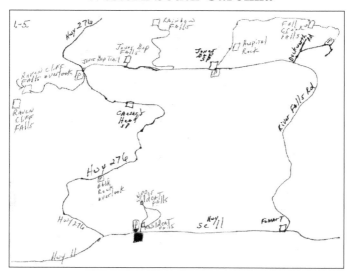

CLEVELAND:
FALLS CREEK FALLS/MOUNTAIN BRIDGE WILDERNESS

Length of Trail: 1.2 miles one way
Condition of Trail: Rugged
Type of Trail: Out and Back
Difficulty of Trail: Strenuous
Approx Hiking Time: 2 hrs
Directions to Trailhead: From Cleveland, SC post office, travel south on hwy 11 for 1 mile. Take a right on River Falls Rd. for 4 miles to Duckworth Rd. Turn right and travel half a mile. Then take a right on Fall Creek Rd for about .4 miles. After Palmetto Bible Camp entrance on right, park on the left at a kiosk and the trailhead.
Trail Description: Take a steep uphill trail 1.2 miles to the falls.

JONES GAP FALLS AT JONES GAP STATE PARK

Length of Trail: 1.2 miles, one way on Jones Gap Trail
Type of Trail: Out and Back
Condition of Trail: Good
Difficulty of Trail: Moderate
Approx Hiking Time: 2 hrs
Directions to Trailhead: From post office in Cleveland take hwy 11 south about a mile. Turn right onto River Falls Rd at F-mart. This road becomes Jones Gap Rd. Follow it 5.5 miles to the end at Jones Gap State Park. Park in parking lot on the right.
Trail Description: Take the Jones Gap Trail # 1, about 1.1 miles, to campsite # 11. Take a right, and follow a spur trail to Jones Gap Falls. Return the way you came.

RAINBOW FALLS AT JONES GAP STATE PARK

Length of Trail: 2.1 miles one way: .5 mile on Jones Gap Trail and
1.6 mile on Rainbow Falls Trail.
Type of Trail: Out and Back
Condition of Trail: Good
Difficulty of Trail: Moderate to Strenuous
Approx Hiking Time: 4 hrs
Directions to Trailhead: From the post office in Cleveland, take
highway 11 south about a mile. Turn right onto River Falls Rd at
F-Mart. This road becomes Jones Gap Road. Follow 5.5 miles to the
end at Jones Gap State Park. Park in parking lot on the right.
Trail Description: Take the Jones Gap Trail for about .5 mile to the
Rainbow Falls Trail on the right. Take the Rainbow Falls Trail 1.6
miles to the base of Rainbow Falls for a total of 2.1 miles one way,
and 4.2 miles round trip. One beautiful waterfall! Return the way
you came.

RAVEN CLIFF FALLS/MOUNTAIN BRIDGE WILDERNESS

Length of Trail: 2 miles one way
Type of Trail: Out and Back
Condition of Trail: Good
Difficulty of Trail: Moderate
Approx Hiking Time: 2-3 hrs
Directions to Trailhead: Take hwy 276 north, approx 1 mile past Caesar's Head State Park. The trailhead is on the right. Park in Raven Cliffs Falls' parking area.
Trail Description: The trail begins across the highway. Take the Raven Cliffs Falls Trail for 2 miles to the observation platform. Return the way you came.

UPPER WILDCAT FALLS

Length of Trail: .4 mile one way
Type of Trail: Out and Back
Condition of Trail: Good
Difficulty of Trail: Easy
Approx Hiking Time: 30 minutes
Directions to Trailhead: From Greenville SC, take hwy 276 north to
the intersection of hwy 11. Continue 4.9 miles north on hwy 276.
Trailhead is at a large paved pull-out on the right.
Trail Description: Take the trail past the Lower Wildcat Falls, which
is roadside. Hike .4 mile to the upper falls. Return the way you
came.

GREENVILLE:
PARIS MT BRISSY RIDGE TRAIL

Length of Trail: 2.4 Miles   Type of Trail: Loop
Condition of Trail: Good   Difficulty of Trail: Strenuous
Approx Hiking Time: 2-2.5 hrs
Directions to Trailhead: From the intersection of hwy 276/291 in
Greenville SC, head east on hwy 291 for .1 mile. Take a left on hwy
253 and go 2. 5 miles. Take a left on State Park Rd and go .8 mile to
Paris Mt. State Park. From the entrance, continue to the Visitor
Center, get a map, and continue up the mountain toward the Brissy
Ridge Trailhead. (Trailhead is also for Sulphur Springs Trail.)
Trail Description: From the trailhead take the Brissy Ridge Trail
where Sulphur Springs and Brissy Ridge Trails split. The other end
of the Brissy Ridge Trail starts at the parking lot. You can go either
way. Taking the Brissy Ridge Trail from the Sulpher Springs/Brissy
Bridge fork gives you a chance to warm up. The trail bears to the
right. Staying on the ridge, take the next intersection, the Kanuga
Trail, to the left. Descend all the way to the road. Cross the road, and
go many ups and downs for a great aerobic workout. This steep part
of the trail is more strenuous than the first part of the trail all the way
back to the parking lot. Trail map marks it in yellow with black dots.

PICKENS:
ESTATOE GORGE TRAIL, SC

Length of Trail: 2.7 miles one way
Type of Trail: Out and Back
Condition of Trail: Good
Difficulty of Trail: Moderate
Approx Hiking Time 3-3.5 hrs
Directions to Trailhead: From the intersection of hwy 178 /hwy 11
north of Pickens, take hwy 178 north for approx 8 miles, passing
through Rocky Bottom, SC and take a left on Horsepasture Rd, just
after the bridge over Estatoe Creek. Look for the Laurel Valley
/Foothills Trail parking area sign. Take Horsepasture Rd .2 mile to
the parking area on the left.
Trail Description: From the parking area, hike up the Horsepasture
Rd west for .2 mile to the sign for the Estatoe Creek Heritage
Preserve Spur Trail on the left. Follow the wide old logging road 1.9
miles to mile 2.1 total, where the trail exits the logging road and
descends for another .6 mile to viewing areas in the gorge at mile
2.7. Go left or right at the sign (indicating The Narrows), for good
views.

RAVEN ROCK AND NATURAL BRIDGE
KEOWEE TOXAWAY STATE PARK

Length of Trail: Approx 5 miles
Type of Trail: Double Loop
Best Direction to Hike: Counter Clockwise
Condition of Trail: Good
Difficulty of Trail: Moderate
Approx Hiking Time: 3-3.5 hrs
Directions to Trailhead: From the intersection of hwy 178/ hwy 11, take
hwy 11 south for about 8.5 miles. Turn right into Keowee Toxaway
State Park. The park office/meeting house will be on your right. The
trail starts behind the parking area at the office.
Trail Description: To walk both loops counterclockwise, stay to
the right at each intersection of trails. Great views of the lake and
open forest.

TABLE ROCK STATE PARK

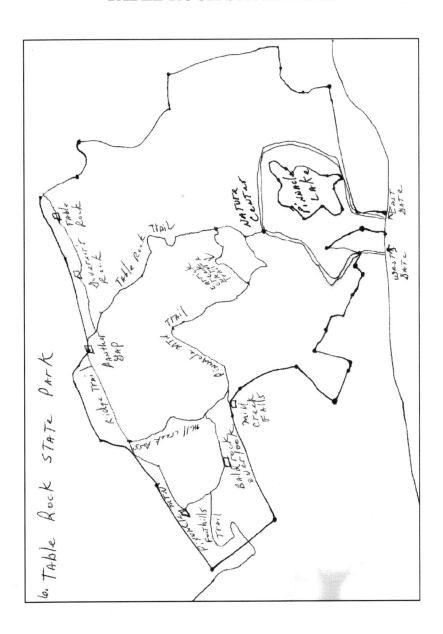

TABLE ROCK TRAIL

Length of Trail: 3.6 miles, one way
Type of Trail: Out and Back
Condition of Trail: Good
Difficulty of Trail: Strenuous
Approx Hiking Time: 4-5 hrs
Directions to Trailhead: From the intersection of hwy 178/
hwy 11, take highway 11 north about 4.1 miles. The Visitor Center/park
office is on the right, directly across the road from the east gate
entrance. After a trip to the Visitor Center/office, enter the east gate and
follow signs to the nature center/parking and trailhead.
Trail Description: From the nature center, follow the Table Rock Trail
3.6 miles to the top.

TWIN FALLS

Twin Falls is off hwy 178, Estatoe Community
Length of Trail: .25 mile one way
Type of Trail: Out and Back
Condition of Trail: Excellent. Well Maintained
Difficulty of Trail: Easy
Approx Hiking Time: 15-20 minutes round trip
Directions to Trailhead: From the Intersection of hwy 178/ hwy 11,
drive 3.2 miles north on hwy 178 to Cleo Chapman Rd on the left at
Bob's Place tavern. Drive 2 miles on Cleo Chapman Road to a T
intersection. Take a right on Eastatoe Community Rd and drive
approx 1 mile. Turn right on Waterfalls Rd, which turns to gravel,
and drive .4 mile, past several private driveways to the end of the
road, to the parking area.
Trail Description: From the parking lot, follow the old roadbed
approx .25 mile to the viewing platform at the falls.

Hiking Trails in
Western South Carolina

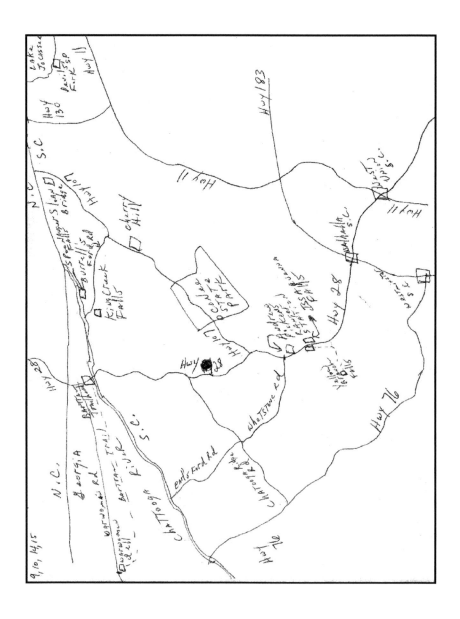

WALHALLA:

ISSAQUEENA FALLS

Length of Trail: About 150 feet from the parking area to the viewing platform. Also, there is a trail to the bottom of the falls.
Type of Trail: Out and Back
Condition of Trail: Excellent
Difficulty of Trail: Easy to viewing platform. Moderate to the bottom of the falls and back.
Approx Hiking Time: 5 minutes to viewing platform. 15 to 20 minutes roundtrip to the bottom of the falls.
Directions to Trailhead: From the intersection of hwy 183/ hwy 28 in Walhalla, SC, drive north on highway 28 for approx 5.5 miles. Turn right into Stumphouse Tunnel Park. Go downhill about a half mile to the picnic area.
Trail Description: Follow the signs to the falls.

KING CREEK FALLS

Length of Trail: Approx .6 mile one way
Condition of Trail: Good
Difficulty of Trail: Moderate
Approximately Hiking Time: About 1 hour roundtrip
Directions to Trailhead: from Walhalla, SC, take hwy 28 northwest for
approx 8 miles to hwy 107. Turn right on hwy 107 north and drive
approx 10 miles to Burrell's Ford Rd. on the left. Take a left on
Burrell's Ford Rd (FS708) and drive 2.4 miles to the Burrell's Ford
Campground parking area on the left.
Trail Description: From the parking area near the information board,
follow the trail (old gravel roadbed) for approx .2 mile. Take a left on
the trail, about 20 yards past an old water pump. Continue for another .2
mile and turn right to cross a bridge over King Creek. Turn left after
footbridge, and go about .1 mile to another intersection indicating
Foothills Trail and King Creek Falls. Go left at the sign indicating King
Creek Falls and walk .1 mile to the falls.

LOWER WHITEWATER FALLS, SC

Length of Trail: 2.4 miles one way
Type of Trail: Out and Back
Condition of Trail: Good
Difficulty of Trail: Moderate
Approx Hiking Time: 2.5 Hours
Directions to Trailhead: From the intersection of SC hwy 130/SC hwy 11, head north toward NC 10.5 miles to the Duke Power Bad Creek Hydro Electric Station on the right. Pass through the automatic gate. Entrance only allowed during daylight hours. Drive 2 miles to the parking area for the Foothills Trail/Whitewater River.
Trail Description: From the trailhead at the end of the parking lot, follow the Lower Whitewater Overlook Spur .7 mile until it crosses the Whitewater River. Take a right after crossing the bridge onto the Jocassee Gorges Foothills Spur. Head northeast on the Foothills Trail .6 mile to the John Garton Spur Trail. Take the John Garton Spur Trail 1.1 miles to the Lower Whitewater Falls Overlook.
**Attention: This trail has been re-routed, making it a little longer out and back.

SPOONAUGER FALLS

Oconee County, SC
Length of Trail: Approx .3 mile one way
Type of Trail: Out and Back
Condition of Trail: Good
Difficulty of Trail: Easy
Approx. Hiking Time: 20-25 minutes roundtrip
Directions to Trailhead: From Walhalla, SC take hwy 28 northwest
for approx 8 miles to hwy 107. Take right on hwy 107 north and
drive approx 10 miles to Burrell's Ford Road on left. Take a left on
Burrell's Ford, FS 708, and drive 2.5 miles to the Burrell's Ford Trail
information sign, at a pull off on both sides of the road. The trail
starts at the information sign.
Trail Description: Follow the Chatttooga River Trail north for .3
mile to the falls.

STATION COVE FALLS

Near Walhalla, SC
Length of Trail: .8 mile one way
Type of Trail: Out and Back
Condition of trail: Good
Difficulty of Trail: Easy
Approximate Hiking Time: 1 hour
Directions to Trailhead: From the Intersection of highway 183/ hwy 11, take hwy 11 north for about 2 miles to Oconee Station Rd on the left. Take Oconee Station Rd a little over 2 miles to a parking area on the left just past the entrance to the Oconee Station on the right. Trail Description: From the trailhead parking area, take the Station Cove Falls Trail .8 mile to the falls. At a little over a half mile, you will come to a fork and a fence. Bear left here to stay on the main trail.

YELLOW BRANCH FALLS

Length of Trail: 1.5 miles one way, .2 mile on the nature trail and 1.3 miles on Yellow Branch Falls Trail.
Type of Trail: Out and Back
Condition of Trail: Excellent. Very well maintained.
Difficulty of Trail: Moderate
Approx Hiking Time: 1.5 hrs
Directions to Trailhead: From the intersection of highway 28/ highway 183, drive north on highway 28 for approx 5.4 miles to Yellow Branch picnic area on your left. Turn left into Yellow Branch picnic area, pass a road to the right, and continue to a large paved parking lot.
Trail Description: Hike .2 mile on the nature trail to the Yellow Branch Falls Trail. Then continue 1.3 miles to the falls.

WESTMINSTER:
BRASSTOWN FALLS CASCADES AND VEIL

Length of trail: .2 mile one way
Type of Trail: Out and Back
Condition of Trail: Good for
cascades; rough for veil; rougher
for sluice not featured here.
Difficulty of trail: Moderate to
Strenuous.
Approx. hiking time: 15 to 20 minutes one way.
Directions to Trailhead: from Westminster, SC, take hwy 76 west for
approx 12 miles to Brasstown Rd. Turn left on Brasstown Road and
drive approx 4.2 miles. (It turns to gravel after 2.7 miles). Turn right
on FS751, just before small bridge, and drive approx .5 mile to the
parking area at the end of the road.
Trail Description: From the parking area, follow the trail past the
vehicle barricade .2 to .3 miles to see all the falls.

BULL SLUICE TRAIL
(On Chattooga River) SC Side

Length of Trail: .2 mile one way
Type of Trail: Out and Back
Condition of Trail: Good
Difficulty of Trail: Easy
Approx Hiking Time: 20-30 minutes depending on how long you
want to enjoy the view.
Directions to Trailhead: Take US hwy 76 northwest from
Westminster, SC for 17 miles to the parking area on the right before
the bridge over the Chattooga River. Park on the SC side.
Trail Description: Follow the paved trail on the left of the
Information Station. Turn right onto the gravel trail and follow .2
mile to the observation platform. Return the way you came.

NARROWS ON THE CHAUGA RIVER

Length of Trail: .6 mile
Type of Trail: Out and
Back
Condition of Trail:
Rough. Old roadbed
becomes very narrow
the further you go in.
Difficulty of Trail:
Moderate
Approx Hiking Time: 45
minutes, round trip
Directions to Trailhead: from Walhalla, SC, take hwy 28 west
approx 7 miles to Whetstone Rd on the left just before Mountain Top
Trading Post. Take a left on Whetstone Rd. for 3.8 miles to
Blackwell Bridge, which crosses the Chauga River. Park on the left
past the bridge in a parking area.
Trail Description: Take the old road bed, which becomes a narrow
fisherman's trail, .6 mile back to the narrows.

REEDY BRANCH FALLS

Length of Trail: Approx .2 mile one way
Type of Trail: Out and Back
Condition of Trail: Good
Difficulty of Trail: Easy
Approx. Hiking Time: Approx 15-20 minutes, roundtrip.
Directions to Trailhead: From Westminster, SC. Take highway 76 northwest for approx 16 miles to Chattooga Ridge Rd on the right. Continue straight on highway 76 another .2 mile and look for pull-out on the left with a gate and a couple of stone pillars. Park in the pull-out beside the road. Be sure not to block the gate.
Trail Description: Walk through the 2 stone pillars and continue .2 mile to the falls.

TENNESSEE

Hiking Trails in
Eastern Tennessee
Overview

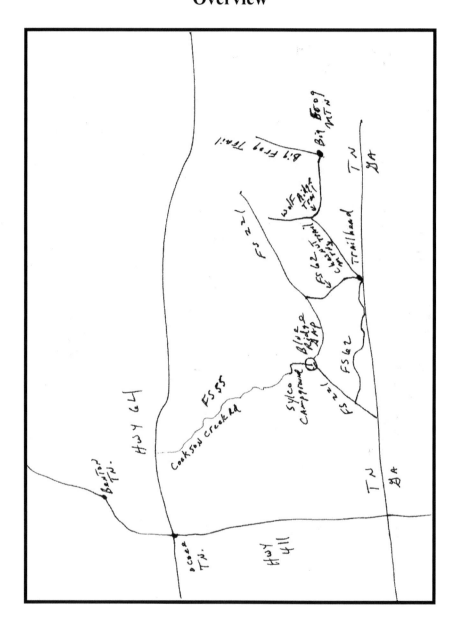

Hiking Trails in
Eastern Tennessee

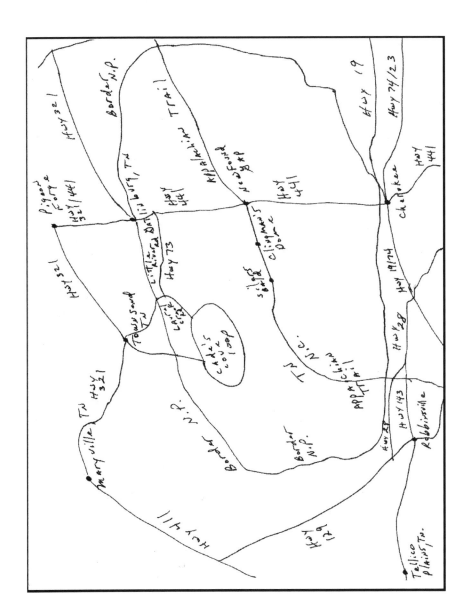

GATLINBURG:
CLINGMANS DOME TO SILERS BALD

Length of Trail: 5 miles one way, 10 miles roundtrip
Type of Trail: Out and Back
Condition of Trail: Rough in some places. Steep climb
Difficulty of Trail: Very Strenuous
Approx Hiking Time: 5-6 hrs
Directions to Trailhead: From the NC/TN state line on hwy 441 at
Newfound Gap, take Clingmans Dome Rd all the way to the end,
approx 7 miles.
Trail Description: Start by following the paved trail to the Clingmans
Dome Tower. After coming down from the tower, take the trail on
the right to the AT. Take a left on the AT, and head south for approx
4.5 miles to Silers Bald from Clingmans Dome, passing Goshen
Prong Trail at 2.6 miles on right, Double Springs Shelter at 3.2
miles, and Welch Ridge Trail to the left at 4.5 miles. A sign at this
junction states "Silers Bald: .4 mile," referring to the shelter. Silers
Bald is only .15 mile away from this intersection.

RAMSEY FALLS (In the Smokies)

Length of Trail: 4 miles one way
Type of Trail: Out and Back
Condition of Trail: Good, except at the 3.5 mile mark: Rough
Difficulty of Trail: Strenuous
Approx Hiking Time 5-6 hrs
Directions to Trailhead: At the junction of 441 and 321 in Gatlinburg
(Traffic Light 3), turn to travel eastbound on 321. Drive 6 miles,
going right into Greenbrier (look for Great Smoky Mountain
National Park entrance sign on the right). This road turns into a
gravel road after a short distance. From Route 321, drive 3.1 miles to
a fork in the road. Turn left here and cross the bridge, and then drive
another 1.5 miles to reach the Ramsey Cascades Trailhead.
Trail Description: After the parking area, the trail turns left and
crosses a wooden footbridge. The first 1.5 miles follows an old
roadbed. At 2.1 miles cross Ramsey Prong on a foot log. At 2.5
miles reach several large trees. At 2.9 miles, reach another foot log
over the stream. From this point the trail gets steeper and at about the
3.5 mile point it is a scramble over rocks and roots, (the most
difficult part of the hike). At 3.9 miles you will have to walk
through the stream over rocks which could be difficult in high water.
Reach Ramsey Cascades at 4.0 miles. Return the way you came.

CHARLIE'S BUNION IN THE SMOKIES

Length of Trail: 3.2 miles one way to the Jump Off. Four miles on AT one way to Charlie's Bunion, approx 9 miles roundtrip for both.
Type of Trail: Out and Back
Condition of Trail: Good
Difficulty of Trail: Strenuous
Approx Hiking Time: 5-6 hrs
Directions to Trailhead: From the Oconaluftee Visitor Center on hwy 441 north of Cherokee, NC, drive approx 15.5 miles north to Newfound Gap. The Appalachian Trail (AT) crosses hwy 441 near the northeastern end of the parking area.
Trail Description: Take the AT north from Newfound Gap parking area. At 1.7 miles, reach the Sweat Heifer Creek Trail to the right. Continue on the AT north to Boulevard Trail at 2.7 miles. Take a left on Boulevard Trail. Go approx .1 mile to the trail on the right to the Jump Off. Continue another .8 mile roundtrip to the Jump Off to the spectacular views of the valley. Backtrack to the AT at 3.7 miles and continue 1.3 miles north on the AT to Charlies Bunion for more spectacular views at 5 miles total. Backtrack south on the AT to Newfound Gap for a 9-mile roundtrip hike.

THE JUMP OFF
and Charlie's Bunion in the Smokies, Continued

OCOEE:

BIG FROG MT.
via Chesnut Mountain/Wolf Ridge Trails

Length of Trail: 3.7 miles one way; 7.4 miles roundtrip
Type of Trail: Out and Back
Condition of Trail: Good
Difficulty of Trail: Strenuous
Approx Hiking Time: 5-6 hrs
Directions to Trailhead: From US hwy 64 /US hwy 411 intersection
near Ocoee, TN, take 64 East approx 2.5 miles before turning right
on Cookson Creek Rd. Cookson Creek Rd does not have a street
sign. Then turn immediately after a gas station, which has signs for
Sylco Campground and Cookson Creek Baptist Church. Take
Cookson Creek Rd 11.5 miles to the FS 55/FS 221 intersection
beyond Sylco Campground. Pavement ends after 4 miles and
becomes FS 55. A half mile after FS 55 becomes dirt/gravel, it bears
to the right, toward Sylco Campground, at a well-marked junction.

BIG FROG MT.
via Chesnut Mountain/Wolf Ridge Trails
Continued

From the 3-way FS 55 -FS 221 intersection. Turn left on FS 221 and go approx 1.8 miles to a right turn on FS 62. Take FS62 (Big Frog Loop Rd). Drive approx 4 miles to the trail sign and make a left turn up into the Chestnut Mt. trailhead parking.
Trail Description: Follow the Chestnut Mt. Trail behind the gate. Go 1.9 miles to the Wolf Ridge Trail. Take a right on the Wolf Ridge Trail and head east 1.8 miles to the top of Big Frog Mountain. Wolf Ridge, Big Frog, and Licklog Ridge Trails all end at the usually-signed high point of the mountain.

TOWNSEND:
ABRAMS FALLS IN THE SMOKIES

Length of Trail: 2.5 miles one way
Type of Trail: Out and Back
Condition of Trail: Good
Difficulty of Trail: Moderate
Approx Hiking Time: 3-3.5 hrs
Directions to Trailhead: The hike to Abrams Falls begins from the
Abrams Falls Trailhead, located at the far western end of Cades
Cove. To reach the trailhead, drive 4.8 miles along the one-way
Cades Cove Loop Road. Just after crossing Abrams Creek, turn right
onto a gravel road. After driving another four-tenths of a mile
through a grassy field, you'll reach a large parking area, where you'll
find signs and a wooden footbridge that marks the trailhead.
Trail Description: From the trailhead, the trail follows Abrams
Creek. At 1 mile reach Arbutus Ridge. The trail descends and then
climbs another ridge at 2 miles. At 2.5 miles, reach a foot log over
Wilson Creek and a side trail leads to Abrams Falls. Return the way
you came.

RICH MOUNTAIN LOOP, TN
Near Cades Cove in the Smokies

Length of Trail: 8.5 miles
Type of Trail: Loop
Condition of Trail: Good
Difficulty of Trail: Moderate to Strenuous, due to the length.

Approx Hiking Time: 4-5 hrs

Directions to the Trailhead: From the Y in Townsend, TN, at the intersection of Little River Rd and TN73, drive on Laurel Creek Rd 7.5 miles to Cades Cove. Park in the large parking lot at the entrance to Cades Cove. The trailhead is just past the gate to Cades Cove Loop Rd, on the right.

Trail Description: From the trailhead, follow the trail .5 mile to the beginning of the loop. The loop combines 3 trails, to make the Rich Mt. Loop Trail: the Crooked Arm Ridge Trail, the Indian Grave Gap Trail, and the Rich Mt. Loop Trail. Take a right on the Crooked Arm Ridge Trail to walk the Loop counter clockwise. At 1.1 miles, reach the ridge crest of Crooked Arm Ridge. At 2.6 miles, reach the intersection with the Scott Mt. Trail on the right. Go straight on the Indian Grave Gap Trail. At 4.3 miles, reach a junction with Rich Mt. Trail on the right. Stay straight on the Indian Grave Gap Trail. At 5.3 miles, reach a junction with the Indian Grave Gap Trail that continues to the right. Turn down to the left, onto The Rich Mt. Loop Trail. The trail starts to descend, and at 7.6 miles you'll reach John Oliver Cabin. At 8 miles, reach the beginning of the loop at the Crooked Arm Ridge Trail. Continue going straight another .5 mile back to the trailhead at 8.5 miles.

SPRUCE FLATS FALLS, Tremont in the Smokies

Length of Trail: 1 mile one way
Type of Trail: Out and Back
Condition of Trail: Good
Difficulty of Trail: Moderate
Approx Hiking Time: 1.5 - 2 hrs
Directions to Trailhead: From the Townsend Y intersection, head
west on Laurel Creek Rd. toward Cades Cove for .2 mile. Take a left
on Tremont Rd, and go 2 miles to the Great Smoky Mountains
Institute on the left. From the parking area at the institute, head down
the road for staff housing and locate the sign that says "Falls" near
the water tower.
Trail Description: Take the falls trail, which is steep at first and then
levels out approx 1 mile to the falls. Go when there has been plenty
of rain. This picture was taken during a dry October.

ABOUT THE AUTHOR

Jack Martin Ellison grew up in Upstate South Carolina and now lives in Birmingham, Alabama, with his wife, Wendy, and their daughter, Blakely. He has a BS in Business Management from the University of Alabama (UAB) and works as a banker.

Ellison enjoys hiking in the Southern Appalachian Mountains every chance he gets, and he is thankful for Jeff Burse for hiking most of these trails with him.

The author hiked every trail in this guide as well as captured the breathtaking photographs featured in each vista with his camera. Vickie Holt, graphics designer of Holt Publishing says, "My father, Leland Hodge, a career professional photographer who worked for the *Herald Journal,* daily newspaper, Spartanburg, South Carolina, taught me through his eyes of perfection the best angles and visual balance. Jack Ellison has a creative eye for excellence, and has delivered a work of art."

Made in the USA
Columbia, SC
22 March 2021